INTELLI⟨

MW01113445

THE FINAL
PROOF OF GOD

By God's Advocate

Dan ANGHEL, M.D.

© Copyright 2016

1

INTELLIGENT DESIGN

THE FINAL
PROOF OF GOD

By God's Advocate

Dan ANGHEL, M.D.

© Copyright 2016

ISBN: 9781520376929

Table of Contents

GOD LOVES YOU

***

GOD DEFENDED THE VICTIMS FROM
THE BEGINNINGS.

***

"GREAT THOUGHTS speak only to the thoughtful
mind but GREAT ACTIONS speak to all mankind."
Theodore Roosevelt.

***

"DON'T BE TRAPPED BY DOGMA - which is living
with the results of other people's thinking."
Steve Jobs.

***

LOVE GOD WITH ALL YOUR MIND.

***

The Holy Infinite Love of God, is our Judge and
Savior, at the same time.

***

Whoever despises the morality of Forgiveness will be
saturated by the Justice.

I have searched a man with a candle during the day like Diogenes, the cynic, and I found Him in Heaven, and His Name is Jesus Christ.

***

A blind man has the liberty to deny the existence of the Sun, but the blind man exists because of the Sun.

***

Whoever despises the law of God, will become a slave of the law of the jungle.

***

God loves the humankind, be humane!

***

The victims from today are yesterday's aggressors, and the victims from The Beginnings were defended by God, even if yesterday the aggressors were in other bodies, in other lives.

***

The truth is the delight of angels and the pain of men.

***

The Holy Infinite Love of God, is our Judge and Savior, at the same time. Be Holy!

***

The one who is perfect in the love for God is made perfect by God.

***

The light is powerful, but the men are blind.

***

The Humanity is our Power, not our weakness.

***

Only small people cannot forgive small mistakes.

***

You cannot be happy because you are naïve, to trust this world and to distrust God.

***

I prefer to be criticized by God, rather than to be loved by men.

***

The love of God is Just, and I just need the love of God.

***

The sky is the same everywhere.
God is the same everywhere and for everybody.

***

Love God with all your mind.

***

To know God, you must first know yourself.

***

The great journeys are made with small steps.

***

I prefer to think that God is right and all humankind is wrong.

***

Christmas doesn't mean cakes, but the love of God.

***

Rejecting God for group conformity is an unforgivable sin.

***

When the arrogance is greater than the will to see, only God can save thee.

***

The Power of the Good Deeds it is the Holy Path to an Invincible Faith.

***

I prefer to think that the whole world deceives itself, and God tells the truth.

***

The best defense is not the offense but the forgiveness, because if you sincerely forgive all you will be forgiven for all, and you will be protected by GOD, like the true victims from The Beginnings.

***

God is every day with us, and we live in Paradise, but He cannot be crucified and worshiped at the same time.

***

I shall not say that I do not know God in the day of His crucifixion, and every day is a day in which the humankind crucifies God by its misjudgment

***

"The light shines into the darkness and the darkness never put it out.". Be light!

***

To control your life, your destiny, you must first control yourself.

***

The imitation of Christ is the imitation of God.

***

Before asking anything from God we must begin by thanking for what we already have.

***

Be sincere in love to receive the sincere love of God.

***

"The collective madness is called sanity." Paulo Coelho

***

"The more a man's life is shaped by the collective norm, the greater is his individual immorality." Carl Gustav Jung

***

The beautiful words can hide dark thoughts, but beautiful thoughts give beautiful feelings.

***

I will prove you that God exists and He is good, and I will also prove you that mankind is evil.

***

"This is the judgment: The Light has come into the world and the men loved the darkness more than The Light because their works were evil" John 3:19

***

The philosophy of darkness is more dangerous than the atomic bomb because it separates us from our protector, God.

This book is a spiritual fight against the philosophy of darkness,

it is the philosophy of light and it will help you to find your way home, into the Light.

God, bless you all, my brothers.

***

Thank you, God, for the rays of light of this day.

***

Thank you, God, for all, and above all thank you!

Scientific Proof of The Existence of God and of the Human Soul

Whoever denies the reason, that proves the existence of God, denies his own sins.

"The Lord is Spirit, and where the Holy Spirit of the Lord is, there is freedom." Corinthians 3:17

"In a world of universal deceit, to tell the truth, is a revolutionary act." George Orwell.

"The MIND OF GOD, we believe, is cosmic music, the music of strings, resonating through 11-dimensional Hyperspace." Michio Kaku

I am a scientist, I am a medical doctor, specialty anesthesia and intensive care, I was educated into the materialistic science, and did not despise it, I used it in order to know the world.

The science and religion actually have the same purpose, to know the truth.

The laws of nature and the "logos", the word of God are actually the same.

The laws that make the galaxies move in an organized way are the "logos", the word of God.

We will begin with what we scientifically know.

We know that the universe and the men are built from atoms and subatomic particles.

According to classical physics, if we theoretically know the position of all particles, atoms in the universe and the laws that govern them, we could theoretically predict the movement of the whole universe and men.

This is called materialistic determinism; it implies that there is no actual free will.

That was a big philosophical dilemma, until the apparition of quantum physics. In our postmodern era, many believe that quantum physics has all the answers, because of the Heisenberg uncertainty principle.

"In quantum mechanics, the uncertainty principle, also known as Heisenberg's uncertainty principle, is any of a variety of mathematical inequalities asserting a fundamental limit to the precision with which certain pairs of physical properties of a particle, known as complementary variables, such as position x and momentum p, can be known simultaneously.

Introduced first in 1927, by the German physicist Werner

Heisenberg, it states that the more precisely the position of some particle is determined, the less precisely its momentum can be known, and vice versa. The formal inequality relating the standard deviation of position σx and the standard deviation of momentum σp was derived by Earle Hesse Kennard later that year and by Hermann Weyl in 1928:

$$\Delta x \Delta p \geq \frac{\hbar}{2}$$

(ℏ is the reduced Planck constant, h / 2π).

Historically, the uncertainty principle has been confused with a somewhat similar effect in physics, called the observer effect, which notes that measurements of certain systems cannot be made without affecting the systems. Heisenberg offered such an observer effect at the quantum level (see below) as a physical "explanation" of quantum uncertainty. It has since become clear, however, that the uncertainty principle is inherent in the properties of all wave-like systems, and that it arises in quantum mechanics simply due to the matter wave nature of all quantum objects. Thus, the uncertainty principle actually states a fundamental property of quantum systems and is not a statement about the observational success of current technology. It must be emphasized that measurement does not mean only a process in which a physicist-observer takes part, but rather any interaction between classical and quantum objects regardless of any observer.

Since the uncertainty principle is such a basic result in quantum mechanics, typical experiments in quantum mechanics routinely observe aspects of it. Certain experiments, however, may deliberately test a particular form of the uncertainty principle as part of their main research program" Wikipedia.

After the invention of quantum physics, the problem of materialistic determinism was solved by the materialistic indeterminism.

Because we cannot know with absolute precision the position of a subatomic particle, that means that the material universe is not absolutely predictable. This doesn't demonstrate that the Human Species is free but only chaotic, the unpredictability doesn't prove the freedom if it depends on the Heisenberg's uncertainty principle.

Because we know also that we are free, and we know that we make conscious decisions, that means that we have another support, "hardware" for the freedom.

The "hardware" that can support a free consciousness cannot be material.

The mechanism that can make possible the freedom it is "a mechanism without mechanism" that I have tried to imagine, and I understood that only God can create something so complex, a mechanism that can make possible the self-determination.

An artificial consciousness, created by men, it is also impossible to create.

Only an infinite Intelligence, can imagine and create the support that can make possible the self-determination.

And the self-consciousness it is even more complex in the nature of its substance.

The "hardware "that can make possible the free consciousness is infinite in complexity, and only a free creative being of infinite intelligence can create it.

Any scientist that says he can create an artificial consciousness is delusional, and only a fool can believe him.

History will prove me right, because in the present there will be many that will pretend they do not understand me, in order to hide from the humanity and from themselves the reality of the existence of God. As Jesus said "The light has come into the world, but people love the darkness rather than the light", and in a genius way Jesus gave also the explanation: ,, because their deeds were evil, for everyone who does what is hateful, hates The Light and does not come to The Light, lest his works should be convicted. But he who does The Truth comes to The Light, so that his works may be revealed".

And God is self-determined by definition.

God is the effect without a cause.

And our profound nature is divine also because our profound nature is the free consciousness, the self-determination.

Because we are free we are self-determined.

The spirit is self-determined, the effect it is without cause, this is the profound nature of God because God is freedom, God is The Creator, and His Profound Nature is the self- determination. We are what came out of God (Exo Deus lat.), we are also self-determined souls, we have the nature of God (Regnum Dei lat.), we are also free and creators.

In the matter:

A------------------------------->B
CAUSE -------------------->EFFECT

In the spirit:

self-determination ----------------->B
self-determination -------------------->EFFECT

B is an effect without a cause
B is self-determined

The EFFECT it is without CAUSE

The EFFECT is self-determined.

Spirit, the Profound Nature of God and Man-----
>EFFECT

God is the effect without a cause, and we are divine in nature because we are free. We are not biochemical robots, we are not just biological machines, we are self-determined consciousness that could only come from God.
This is logical.

And this is the profound reason for what God does not make the decisions for us, He lets us make our own decisions, because, we are by Nature self-determined, we are like Him, Regnum Dei not Regnum Animalis.
In the material world, A determines B
In the spiritual world, B is self-determined, there is no cause for B, and this is the Profound Nature of God and of all the souls that came out of God.
Actually, the souls are sustained into existence because of the will of God. We exist because God sustains our consciousness and freedom, our spiritual and physical bodies.

We exist because God loved us into existence, and He loves us because we were born, and we were born of Him, of the Original self-determined and creator spirit, the Spirit of the Truth, the Holy Spirit.

The origin of our actions, words, and thoughts, of the will, is the self-determination, it is in and through the nature of our souls, that have the same Nature as the Nature of God. We are Regnum Dei, we are not Regnum Animalis, as our current science says.

Einstein said in his book, the Theory of relativity for all, that "we cannot will to will ".

Actually, he was very close of the understanding of the Nature of God and of the souls, but he didn't understand, because he stayed in the

paradigm of materialism, he imagined other dimensions and the

quantum physic imagine also other dimensions other parallel universes, but they stay in the "box" of materialism, of determinism or the chaotic subatomic indeterminism, but they reject the idea that it is a dimension, a "universe" where not the laws of physics rule, but the will of the souls, not the exterior determinism, but the interior self-determinism.

There is a parallel universe and it is self-determined, it is called, God and the souls that came out of God.

The matter cannot support hardware, even of infinite complexity, that can have a self- determined consciousness, and it is empirically proven that we are self-determined consciousness. For example, a very similar group of people do not behave the same in various psychological experiments, in the same conditions. There is a majority that behaves in a predictable manner, but not all. And this is the empirical demonstration that we are free.

The Nature of The "hardware" that can support the freedom and consciousness it is so complex, that there is no human mind that can imagine it, even Einstein when he said we "cannot will to will" ...we simply will...and the origin of the will is in our divine Nature. We are Regnum Dei, not Regnum Animalis.

You cannot do human medicine if you only studied veterinary medicine, you can understand some things, you can brutally treat some diseases, but you absolutely cannot understand all the human medicine by only studying veterinary medicine.

In the same way with applying our quantum physics into understanding God.
Only God could imagine and determine the self-determination, He is self-determined, He is the effect without a cause, and we have His Divine Nature, we can also create effects without cause, and this is what unites us, the possibility of creation, of choice.

Freedom is the Profound Nature of God.

We are not biological, biochemical robots. Our consciousness is not an epiphenomenon of our biochemical machine that we call body, our consciousness it is not just a spectator of the movement of our biological machine, that we call the body.

Our consciousness is interconnected with the freedom and they are both divine in Nature.

Some of us depend on the void logic of mathematics, I relay on the live logic of common sense.

The Heisenberg uncertainty principle does not demonstrate the liberty but the chaos. If a system is unpredictable it means that is chaotic or self-determined.

And the Human Species is self-determined

We are an immortal nucleus of free consciousness and we have the same profound Nature as the profound Nature of God.

And this is the reason why God doesn't make the decisions for us because if He would that meant that we wouldn't be free.

We came of God, we are pieces of God, we are free and immortal, supra-materialistic. Our bodies are just biological robots that were given to us from God, it is our choice if we want or not to live on autopilot.

It is the free immortal consciousness, our soul, that controls the biological machine, that we call the body.

After the invention of quantum physics, the problem of materialistic determinism was solved by the materialistic indeterminism.

Because we cannot know with absolute precision the position of a subatomic particle, that means that the material universe is not absolutely predictable. This doesn't demonstrate that the Human Species is free but only chaotic, the unpredictability doesn't prove the freedom if it depends on the Heisenberg's uncertainty principle.

Because we know also that we are free, and we know that we make conscious decisions, that means that we have another support, "hardware" for the freedom.

Because we are free we are self-determined.

God is the effect without a cause. He is self-determined.

And we are to self-determined because we are free, ergo we have the same nature with God...
We came out of God, we came out of the Father of lights, we simply created the darkness.
Because we are free, we can also make effects without a cause.

Because God is Absolute in Good, Truth, and Beauty, it implies logically that we are the only responsible for our destiny.

Because we are self-determined, we are powerful and responsible, the masters of our own destiny.

God is Spirit, and where the Holy Spirit of God is, there is freedom.

God is freedom, in the absolute superior form of organization.

God is The Creator, and the superior form of organization of freedom is the creation. And we are not only matter , superior organized like the atheist materialist say, but we came out of God, and we were given by God, the supreme gift of freedom and creation.

We are parts of God, our spirit exists because He sustains us into existence, even when we crucify Him by our mistakes, He continues to love us.

The love of God, sustains us into existence, even when we use our freedom in an arrogant way.
Because we are free there must be a support, hardware for the self-determination.

In the classical physics A det. B

In the quantum physics A det. B

or A det. C

In the spirit :
B it is self-determined

There is no cause for B

The structure of the soul cannot be imagined by the human mind.
It is a mechanism without a mechanism.

This is the truth and God cannot be lied to.
This is the testimony of a saved soul by Jesus Christ.

I will not say that I do not know Christ, as someone in the Bible before His Crucifixion, because I know Him, and He knows me better than I know myself, and He knows you also better then you want to know yourself.
But Socrates said "know yourself " and Jesus said, " you shall know the truth and the truth will make you

free". And when you will have the courage to see yourself beyond your mistakes you will find in you, God.

God lives in you, live also in God, through God, and for God, by doing His Holy Will. Use your self-determination in a wise and good way, because any way that doesn't lead to God, leads to darkness.

I shall not say that I do not know God in the day of His crucifixion, and every day is a day in which the humankind crucifies God by its misjudgment.

It took a man, not a machine, to find the truth.

The artificial free consciousness is a utopia.

The Solution to the problem of evil

"It is your eye evil because I am good?" GOD, Mat. 20:15

"Who controls the past controls the future, and who controls the present controls the past." George Orwell

We all devolved from higher purer humanity, that had, in the beginning, a divine identity, a born divine nobility. We were human-divine and from divine humanity. In the beginning, God created all perfect in body and spirit.

And because of the rebellion against the morality of God we devolved.

We created another morality, but it was proven to us wrong.

I advise you to return to the morality of God, who is forgiveness and holy love of any soul that came out of Him.
I did that and He made me as I was in the beginning, God cleansed me in His own blood, so I am clean.

Now we know that God exists.
And it is logical that God loves His creation.
This is common sense logic.

23

God loves all the souls that came out Him as He loves Himself. We are parts of God, we cannot exist separated from Him, we think we left Him but He never left us.

God loves the Human Species.

All the souls because they are self-determined, they have the same nature as the nature of God. We are all parts of God, we were born of God, and God loves us because we were born.

God not only created us, but He sustains us into existence, by never stopping to love us, even when we crucify Him by our mistakes, by our bad thoughts, by our misjudgment.

And we know that we are self-determined and responsible for our own lives.

The philosophical problem of evil tormented me for years. I was obsessed with this problem.

And I solved it, the solution is: The victims from today are yesterday's aggressors, and the victims from the beginning were defended by God, even if yesterday the aggressors were in other bodies, in other lives.

The demonstration of the existence of reincarnation:
The premise: GOD IS JUST
Conclusion: we all deserve our fate: we pay for sins from past lives.

Because GOD IS JUST, we deserve our pain, and we pay sins from past lives. This explains why some of us are born to suffer, actually, they are born to pay because in another life they made another person suffer.

Anybody who doesn't believe in reincarnation and he says he believes that God is just, lies. It is logical for any non-dogmatic free mind.

That means that every victim from today, is an aggressor from yesterday, even that yesterday he was in another body.

The today's victims are yesterday's aggressors, and the victims from the beginning were defended by God.

God loves the Human Species.

God loves you because you were born!
Receive God's, Holy Love!

BUT WHAT HAPPENED WITH THE VICTIMS FROM THE BEGINNING?
THEY WERE DEFENDED BY GOD.

The beginning it is the first civilization.
When God created the Human Species, He created it perfect.
The first civilization was very spiritually and technological developed.
We were born from the Perfect One.
At the beginning we really felt our Born Divine Nobility, we felt and accepted our divine identity.

We were one with God, but humble in God's Holy Spirit, we were humble in front of God.

The Beginning

Aggressors -------------->Victims
The victims, from the Beginning, were defended by God

Past

reincarnated Aggressors with sins to pay,
the fall of Atlantis= the flood of Noah=tsunami

Present
Aggressors, that believe that they are Victims

"For Christ also suffered for sins once for all, the righteous for the unrighteous, to bring you to God. He was put to death in the body, but made alive in the spirit, in which He also went and preached to the spirits in prison who disobeyed long ago when God waited patiently in the days of Noah, while the ark was being built." Peter (1, 3:18-20).

"But they deliberately overlook the fact that long ago by God's word the heavens existed and the earth was formed out of the water and by water, through which the world of that time perished in the flood. And by that same word, the present heavens and earth are reserved for fire, kept for the day of judgment and destruction of ungodly men...."Peter (2,3:5-7)

The Apostol Peter said that "they deliberately overlook" because as our savior Jesus Christ said: "This is the judgment: The Light has come into the world and the children of men loved the darkness more than The Light because their works were evil. For everyone who does what is hateful, hates The Light and does not come to The Light, lest his works should be convicted. But he who does The Truth comes to The Light, so that his works may be revealed, that they are performed by God." (John 3).

If you realize that you are an old aggressor, reincarnated, and God is really good, if you repent and forgive all, the blood of God, of Jesus Christ, can clean you and make you like the victims from the beginning, and you will be protected by The Holy Spirit like the victims from the beginning.

The Holy Trinity wants to help us.
We just must see that we are the evil ones, not God.
If you think you are an innocent victim and you suffer unjustly you make a Sin Against the Spirit of the Truth, and you are not in the truth.

Let's assume that a serial killer makes a stroke and forgets all that he has done, even believes that he is as innocent as a child.

Let's assume that nobody knew he was a murderer, and that he succeeded before the stroke to hide his traces.

Then he is hospitalized in a top university clinic where is treated by the most famous professors in neurology.

In the day of divine justice, the murderer and the professors believed that he suffered unjustly, that the destiny was unjust with the poor man.

They all are guilty of the sin of unbelief and they are out of paradise.

But the serial killer will suffer more than the professors.

But the disbelief of the teachers will not go unpunished also, because you see: he was a murderer and he must be punished.

In the same way with this prison planet.

Some of them are murderers and suffer greatly, some of them are unbelievers and suffer less, but they all suffer: because they offend The God of Love, assuming that He is unjust.

And everyone deserves their karma and the victims from the beginning were defended by God.

But why the professors, men, and women with deep minds who understood the complexity of the brain could not understand the goodness, the justice and the love of God?

Simply, I answer: because of the very high image of themselves that they had because they too had made mistakes.

Because whoever exalts himself will be humbled, and he who humbles himself will be exalted.

So, it is with the ones who want to forget that they are born again, some for life some for death.

Because GOD IS JUST, we deserve our pain, and we pay sins from past lives. This explains why some of us are born to suffer, actually, they are born to pay because in another life they made another person suffer.

The victims from today are yesterday's aggressors, and the victims from the Beginning were defended by God.

In the beginning, God created us all good, perfect in body and spirit.

We all had the Born Nobility of God.

We all of any race or color have devolved from the angelic state of the first divine men, that were in communion with the Holy Spirit.

Ecce Homo (Behold the man): Jesus Christ, who showed us the true face of God, the true morality and power of the Light.

I have searched a man with a candle during the day like Diogenes, the cynic, and I found Him in Heaven, and His Name is Jesus Christ.

Jesus Christ is the True Image of God and of the True men from the beginning.

And the key to the gate of Heaven is Repentance and Forgiveness through Jesus Christ, our divine savior.

We are all, indifferent of nationality or race, the descendants of a Higher and purer Humanity that came out of God.

This is logical because:

GOD IS JUST AND GOD IS LOVE.

So: THE LOVE OF GOD IS OUR JUDGE.

And some of us have fallen some of us have not.

The known Human Species is an involution from the Initial Human Species that had the Born Nobility of God.

Actually in the eyes of the Holy Spirit the actual Human Species it is Posthuman, had lost the divine nobility from the beginning and had lost actually the humanity itself.

Ecce Homo(Behold the man): Jesus Christ.

We belong not to the animal kingdom (regnum animalis) but to God's Kingdom (Regnum Dei).

But, attention my friends: who despises the law or the word of God will be let to the law of the jungle.

"Who controls the past controls the future, and who controls the present controls the past" George Orwell

References of reincarnation in the Bible:

Archangel Gabriel:

"And he (John the Baptist) shall go before God, in the spirit and power of Elias" Luke 1:17

"And his disciples asked him, saying: Why then do the scribes say that Elias must come first?

But he answering, said to them: Elias indeed shall come, and restore all things.

But I say to you, that Elias has already come, and they knew him not, but have done unto him whatsoever they had a mind. So also the Son of man shall suffer from them.

Then the disciples understood, that he had spoken to them of John the Baptist." Mat. 17:10

Jesus Testimony

8 May 2005
The Passover of both orthodox and catholic Christians.

"Whoever exalts himself will be humbled, and whoever humbles himself will be exalted." (Mat. 23:12)

It was night and I was in my bed,

I repented for all my sins, and sincerely said to God that I forgive all that ever sinned against me from the beginning of my creation, from all my past lives and from the present life. I had this very important thought:

GOD DEFENDED THE VICTIMS FROM THE BEGINNING.

It was the solution to the problem of evil, a problem from that I was obsessed for years.

And I saw a star descending from Heaven into my room, I felt a divine presence, and I knew it was Jesus Christ.

Through me started to progressively flow a river of Holy Divine

Love, and I knew the source of the river of love was an infinite ocean. And I became the Infinite Ocean of Holy, Pure Infinite Love.

And God loves every one of us with the same Infinite Holy Love, but the humankind has its heart closed in arrogance.

I thought: I do not deserve so much love, I am a sinner.
And God said to me: I LOVE YOU BECAUSE YOU WERE BORN.

Jesus made me as I was at the beginning.
Jesus made me like a victim from the beginning, although I am an aggressor, from the beginning.
He gave me back my lost divine soul.
In this book, I have proven, so that your reason can understand, not only the justice of God but also His Love.
But to receive His sincere infinite love you must have a sincere heart with God, yourself and your brothers and sisters.
Return to God!

***

In a dream, God revealed Himself to me:
He was crucified in a perfect blue sky,
His skin was like a combination of the color of all the races in the world, but a little dehydrated like a dehydrated apple.
He was full of Holy Infinite love.

He had a wound at a foot, an open wound, and He loved me also through that wound.

He had a slight smile for me, from the Cross.

He was not at all sad or in suffering as a human would be.

The Holy Infinite Love that He has for us actually dilutes the pain of the Cross. His eyes were big, of infinite Holy beauty a mix of blue and green.

His Face was emanating power and goodness.

His Face didn't show any sign of pain, only Holy Love.

And He said to me, with a slight smile:

I AM CRUCIFIED FOR YOUR EVERY MISTAKE!

I KNEW THAT HE WAS THE CREATOR SPIRIT OF THE UNIVERSE.

The Philosophy of Light

"Who loves forgives and who forgives loves." God's
Advocate

*God, bless you all, my brothers and sisters from The
Beginnings!*

"The Light shines in the darkness, and the darkness
never put it out" John 1:5
***

The truth is the delight of angels and the pain of men.
***

A blind man can deny the existence of the Sun, but the
blind man exists because of the Sun
***

Whoever denies the reason, that proves the existence of
God, denies his own sins.
***

Whoever despises the morality of forgiveness, will be
saturated by the justice.
***

The best defense is not the offense but the forgiveness,
because if you sincerely forgive all you will be forgiven
for all, and you will be protected by GOD, like the true
victims from The Beginnings.
***

The Holy Infinite Love of God, is our Judge and
Savior, at the same time. Be Holy!
***

Whoever despises the law or the word of God, will become a slave of the law or the lies of the jungle.
***

The Humanity is our Power, not our weakness.
***

"A man who doesn't believe in God is an animal who comes from nowhere and goes nowhere." Constantin Noica, philosopher
***

Heaven means eternal gratitude.

If you will sincerely thank God for every sunshine of every morning, you will be every morning in Paradise.

For the Paradise is like an eternal calm full of peaceful light, morning.
***

The difference between heaven and hell is just a thought.
***

Only small people cannot forgive small mistakes.
***

A House divided cannot stand.
***

The ordinary vessel doesn't go often to the water but the vessel of God goes as many times as he wants to the water.

God is an Infinite Ocean of Holy Love, Truth, and Goodness.
***

Don't be naïve, the beautiful words can hide dark thoughts, but the beautiful thoughts give beautiful feelings.

***

You cannot be happy because you are naïve, to trust this world and to distrust God.

***

The people are like stained glass.

There are some that are completely dark and the light does not cross them or do not enter them.

There are ones that are dirty and the light that crosses them gets out dirty also.

And there are those who have beautiful colors and the light that crosses them is very beautiful.

And there are those who are completely transparent, sincere in front of God, and the light that crosses them is perfect like the light that entered them.

Jesus reflected exactly the light of God and His words are exactly the words of God.

Be not deceived by the dirty minds, that taint the TRUTH.

***

"Christianity is a religion too noble, for a being so ignoble as the man."

Soren Kierkegaard

***

The one who is perfect in the love for God is made perfect by God.

***

It has no importance what you think about me, but it is of the highest importance what we think about God, and this is our judgment.

***

Cleanse me, My God!

Above the dark clouds of our bad thoughts, the sky is always blue.

***

The Thoughts of God will make us CLEAN and FREE.

***

A real tragedy would be to be in the prison of sin and to believe that you are free.

***

Over the clouds, the sky is always blue.

***

The nostalgia of sin felt sometimes by the angels, and always by the mediocrity.

***

In THE BEGINNING, we were a highly-advanced civilization, much more advanced than we are today, morally and technologically.

We had the Born Nobility of the Holy Spirit of God in us.

We were a superior race in comparison with what we are today. All the races of this world are the descendants of a better world, a better man, that was created exactly in the spirit and power of God.

This is the new THEORY OF HUMAN DEVOLUTION.

And this planet has fallen when it rebelled against the Holy Spirit of God, and the Sin against the Holy Spirit shall not be forgiven, not then, not now, not in the future.

In THE BEGINNING, WE WERE CREATED AFTER THE

IMAGE OF GOD BUT THE HUMANITY DESECRATED THE
IMAGE OF GOD, THAT LIVED AND STILL LIVES IN US, AND THE TRUE IMAGE OF THE ONE TRUE GOD IS JESUS CHRIST.

WHOEVER DESPISES THE MORALITY OF FORGIVENESS WILL BE
SATURATED BY THE JUSTICE
***

"This world will pass, but my words will never pass."
Jesus Christ.
***

The humanity from today it is just a sick and crippled shadow of HUMANITY FROM THE BEGINNING.

The humanity before the rebellion had a born divine nobility, given by the communion with God, and noblesse obliges to make only divine, good deeds.

We were a superior race, we were perfect angels, pure in spirit and in the body. Human-divine and from divine humanity.

But the humanity desecrated the image of God that lived and still lives in us, and the True Image of the One True God is Jesus Christ.
***

God loves you,

But you are a prodigal son,
Return Home, God misses you.

This book will show you the way Home, into the Light of God: Jesus Christ the Truth, The Life, and the Path.
***

The men swim in an ocean of sweet water, and they say that they die of thirst, because they were lied that the water is salty, and they fear to drink it.

Fear not, because GOD IS LOVE.
***

THE SKY IS THE SAME OVERALL.
THE SKY IS THE SAME EVERYWHERE AND OVER ALL. AND ABOVE THE CLOUDS OF OUR DARK THOUGHTS THE SKY IS ALWAYS BLUE.
***

The root of evil it is in the spiritual mediocrity!
Because the sin produces the self-deception that fuels our pathological ego.
***

Whoever despises the law of God will become a slave of the law of the jungle.
***

I am soft with them, but they are rough against God.
That's why I shall not spare them from the Truth.
***

To be saved you must not have the faith of the old ladies, but the faith of angels!
***

When the arrogance is greater the will to see, only God can save thee.
***

Only when you see and condemn the darkness in you, can you see the Goodness of GOD.

***

"The judgment it is without mercy for the ones who showed no mercy." James 2:13.

***

The Forgiveness, The Love and The Justice of God do not contradict themselves.

The ones who forgive will be forgiven, and therefore logically protected. The ones who love with a sincerely, holy love will receive the Love of God.

And the ones who cry out for justice will receive justice ...

***

When the evil becomes a banality, we believe that is innocent. It is not innocent, just mediocre.

***

The love of God,

The majority cannot feel it because they are just flowers who are too young or they are too old...already dead spiritually.

***

You must clean the feet of your brothers of the dirt of this world if you want God to cleanse you.

Remember what Jesus said: „It is sufficient if the disciple is like his

Teacher". If He cleaned our feet, we must also clean one another's feet.

***

The greatest sin is to think you have no sin.

***

The light is powerful, but the men are blind.
***

A madman can watch the sun, through a filthy glass and believe that his rays are dirty, and only another madman will believe him.

And this madness is a sin against the Holy Spirit and the present state of the collective consciousness of humanity.

We must cleanse our collective consciousness.
***

This verse is a reminder for our prayers:

Forgive us our trespasses as we forgive the ones who trespassed against us. (Lord's Prayer)

We do not need to remind God to be merciful:
He is, He was and He will always be merciful.
We must remind ourselves to be merciful, and to forgive our enemies, to receive the mercy of God, and to be forgiven.
It is mandatory to forgive if you want to be forgiven.
God is Truth and in Him, it is no lie at all, so if we want to have a good relationship with God, we must begin of being truthful with Him.
The hypocrites are the sons of darkness, and from the beginning, God separated the darkness from the light.
***

GOD IS WITH ME, AND I AM NOT AGAINST HIM.
***

Rejecting God for group conformity is an unforgivable sin.

***

If a prisoner knows he is guilty, he will stay in prison, will not be liberated earlier.

That's why we need to repent and forgive.

And God, is such a loving person, that if He sees true repentance and true forgiveness, he will make the prisoner free because he is no longer a predictable danger to society.

And we cannot deceive God.

***

God is every day with us, and we live in Paradise.
But He cannot be crucified and worshiped at the same time.

***

God loves the Human Species.
When God descended on this prison planet, the inmates crucified Him, and He proved the infinite love that He has for this decayed humanity.

***

We make the great voyages with small steps.
Decide yourself to know God, and He will have patience with you. You will need the provisions of good acts, words, and faith.

***

Jesus always begins His prayers by thanking God.

***

God is love, and you can understand Him only through true love, and this cannot be taught in a book by words, it is a choice you make with your heart.

***

The Cross is the ultimate evidence of the love of God for the humankind.

The men crucify God daily in their minds, by misjudging Him, and this is for God equally painful as the pain of the physical Cross, from 2000 years ago.

***

The justice, the forgiveness, the mercy and the love of God do not contradict themselves.

We are forgiven if we forgive.

We receive mercy if we are merciful.

And we must be holy, to receive the Holy infinite love of God.

***

"We should obey God rather than man" Acts 5:29.

***

God is with me, and I am not against Him.

***

God loves the humankind!

Be humane!

***

"Anyone who hates his brother is a murderer." 1 John 3:15.

***

"God is light, and in Him, there is no darkness at all." 1John 1:5.

***

"Jesus is the same yesterday, today and forever."
Apostle Paul
(Hebrews 13:8)
***

"The light shines into the darkness, and the darkness
never put it out." John 1:5
***

"If we say that we have no sin, we deceive ourselves,
and the truth it is not in us "1 John 1:8
***

"If we say we haven't sinned, we make God a liar, and
His word it is not in us." 1 John 1:10.
***

"Only God is good." Jesus Christ (Luke 18:19)
***

But whoever hates his brother is in the darkness and
walks in the darkness, and does not know where he is
going, because the darkness has blinded his eyes." 1
John 2:11
***

The Power of the Good Deeds it is the Holy Path to an
Invincible Faith.

I will explain myself: we can be tempted to love the
darkness in order to hide from ourselves, in the abyss of
the subconscious, the evil deeds. So never to be tempted
by the darkness we absolutely need to be powerful
through the richness of the good deeds.
***

The Human Species wakes up only to dream a
nightmare that it likes.

The Humankind believes it is morally superior to God
because:

1. Falsely believes it is a victim of God.

2. Disrespects Jesus, who reflected exactly the morality of God, which is the forgiveness.

And this false believe it is a sin against the Spirit of the Truth.

***

Whoever despises the morality of forgiveness will be saturated by the justice.

***

To understand why the best defense is not the offense but the forgiveness:

If you forgive all, you will be forgiven for all and you will be protected like the angels, like the victims from The Beginnings. You will be equal to angels and made clean by the Blood of God, and we must not name unclean what God cleansed with the Blood of His Beloved Son.

This is the key that Jesus promised Peter: You shall not name unclean what God made clean, with His Blood.

***

-If you have a son who made a crime and he must go to prison You will stop loving your son?

-No, you will probably love him more.

-But, you know that he deserves the prison.
And you will do anything to liberate him.

God does everything to liberate us.

God will forgive us if we forgive also our brothers.

Because He loves us all with the same infinite love, He loved our victim with the same love He loves us, and He protected the true victims from the beginning.
***

Any lie that makes you doubt the love of God is more dangerous than the atomic bomb if you believe it.
"I tell the Truth, that's why you do not believe me "
Jesus Christ
***

God loves us.

In the same way, somebody despised your love, in the same way, you despise the love of God.

Believe not that you are morally superior to God.
Believe not that you are a victim of God.

Believe not that your morality is superior to the morality of the Cross, to the morality of Christ.

Because the morality of Christ is the morality of God, and it is a historical fact that God is our victim.
***

Be rich in good deeds, words, and thoughts and you shall never fear the light, and you shall never hide in the shadow of the lying trees.

We are all naked of secrets in front of God.
***

The truth will make us free because the lies made us slaves.
***

I prefer to think that the whole world deceives itself, and God tells the truth.

***

If a whole planet says a foolish thing, it is still a foolish thing. I speak about the bad faith.

***

Who doesn't respect the truth, respects not God.

And the historical truth it is that when God descended on Earth we crucified Him, not Him us!

We must become doers of the law from readers of the law to stay in Paradise.

***

Divide not, and be not divided against God!

***

The perspective of the Holy Spirit.

Be holy, honest with yourself, God and your brothers, to have the perspective of paradise, of angels, of the men from the beginning.

***

When the evil becomes a banality, we believe that is innocent. It is not innocent, just mediocre.

***

The fear of God is the beginning of wisdom.

The love of God is the completeness of wisdom.

***

The best defense is not the offense but the forgiveness

***

God loves you, but you are an adulterous soul, that left the Spirit of the Truth for an arrogant illusion.

***

God loves you but you are to Him unfaithful.
***

We live in the light, but we close our eyes because we do not want to see our mistakes.
***

Our thoughts will save us,
In the same way, our thoughts destroyed us.
***

The absolute power is the Power of Light of Jesus Christ.
***

Do not beg from beggars: love or respect!

Instead, take freely from God love and respect!
***

"What is the Truth?" Pilate (John 18:38)
"The truth is the Word of God." Jesus Christ (John 17:17)
***

Has no importance what you believe about me, but what we believe about God, and this is our judgment.
***

God is with me and I am not against Him.
***

If you are politically correct, you are a slave of this world.

If you are divinely correct, you shall become a Son of God.
***

The human species became post-human, despising the love the truth and the path of God.

And whoever despises the law of God will become a slave of the law of the jungle, a "mechanical animal" as Descartes said.

***

We shall never forget that the priests (Pharisees) and intellectuals

(scribes) crucified God, and they still do, in the spirit.

***

It is strange how we can thank a stranger for a cup of coffee, but we cannot thank God for the vessel of life.

***

If you have an infected foot, the head cannot say:

"I do not care, I am fine."

The head must treat the foot so the whole body will survive.

So, it is with the Humankind: we must be merciful.

***

Thank you, Lord for the gift of life.

Thank you, God, for all your gifts.

God, please, in the Name of Jesus Christ, cleanse the collective consciousness of the humankind from the blasphemous lies of this world.

Thank you!

***

The best defense is not the offense, but the forgiveness.

***

I prefer to be criticized by God, rather than to be loved by man.

***

If you love God with all your mind you will enter Paradise.

Avoid not the hard questions!

By this will know the truthful answers: the Truth never blasphemes God.

***

I prefer to think that the whole world is wrong, and God is right.

***

God is with me, and I am not against Him. I will always be God's Advocate. And in this way, I will protect myself, because God lives in me, God lives in us.

***

God loves us with all our errors.

We function by the algorithm of trial and error.

But if we refuse to see our errors, we will forever fail. God is light, be not blind!

The ones who refuse to see God in all His beauty, are the ones who prefer to stay blind to their mistakes.

God tells always the truth, that's why some of us do not love Him, because they do not love what the truth says about themselves.

"God is light, and in Him is no darkness at all." (1John 1:5)

***

Before asking anything from God we must begin by thanking for what we already have, a free immortal consciousness.

***

The art of true living is the art of true, sincere, holy love.

"Be holy as God is Holy." (1Peter 1:16).

Be sincere in love to receive the sincere love of God.
***

Beware of the love of men, because the men do not know how to love, and when they love, they love towards death.

Search the love of God, because the love of God is the eternal life.

Trust in the love of God.

Stay in the love of God.

Believe in the love of God.

Despise not the love of God.

Open your mind and heart to the love of God.

Be the love of God.

Because:
"Love is patient, love is kind. It does not envy, it does not boast, it is not proud. It is not rude, it is not self-seeking, is not easily angered, it keeps no account of wrongs. Love takes no pleasure in evil but rejoices in the truth. It bears all things, believes all things, hopes all things, endures all things. Love never fails." (1Corinthiens 13:4).

Because also:

"If I speak in the tongues of men and of angels, but have not love, I am only a ringing gong or a clanging cymbal. If I have the gift of prophecy and can fathom all mysteries and all knowledge, and if I have absolute faith so as to move mountains, but have not love, I am nothing. If I give all I possess to the poor and exult in the surrender of my body, but have not love, I gain nothing. "(Corinthians 13:1).

**

We shall learn the science of God, and to scientifically understand God we must use our minds and our hearts also.

***

The Holy Infinite Love of God is our Judge.

***

The vessel goes not often to the water

But the vessel of God goes how many times he wants to the water.

***

"The wisdom is proved right by all her children." Jesus Christ

***

Return to your first love: The Spirit of the Truth.

***

Do not beg from beggars, love or respect.
Just thank God for all.

***

The most dangerous soul in hell is the one who believes he is an angel, who has forgotten he has fallen.
And this soul is the soul of man.

***

When Jesus said: "Eli, Eli lama sabactani?"

He was referring to us.

We left Him.

GOD NEVER LEFT JESUS AND HE WILL NEVER
LEAVE US.
We left Him, like arrogant adulterous souls (unfaithful).

God sustains us into existence, He sustains our free
immortal consciousness, who is a part of Him. Without
Him loving us, we cannot exist.

And He will love us indifferent of our mistakes, how
He already revealed by His Crucifixion.
***
Who loves forgives,
Who loves not, forgives not.

And who forgives will be forgiven by God.

Buddha never said that Buddha just said that we must
pretend that the pain doesn't exist.
It exists and it is a proof and a fuel of our arrogance.
***
Whoever Despises the Morality of Forgiveness will be
Saturated by the Justice.
***
The sky is the same everywhere.
God is the same everywhere and for everybody.
***
Any lie that makes you doubt the love of God, offends
the Holy Spirit.

This lie is more dangerous than the atomic bomb if you believe it.
***

"If a blind leads a blind, they will all fall into Abyss."
Jesus Christ.
***

Whoever denies the existence of God, denies his own sins.
***

The humanity is not our weakness but our power!
***

"And forgive us our trespasses, as we forgive those who trespass against us." Lord's Prayer

GOD SAID WE MUST FORGIVE TO BE FORGIVEN.
WE MUST BE MERCIFUL TO RECEIVE MERCY.
THE MAJORITY IGNORE THIS TRUTH.
***

GOD IS WITH ME, AND I AM NOT AGAINST HIM.
***

"I send you to testify about me, to open their eyes and to bring them from darkness to light..." Jesus to Paul. (Acts 26:18)
***

The beautiful words can hide dark thoughts

But the beautiful thoughts give beautiful feelings.

By their fruits, you shall know the trees.
***

It has no importance what you think about me, but it is of the highest importance what we think about God, and this is our judgment.

The difference between heaven and hell it is simply the degree of respect that we have for God.

Every thought has attached a feeling.

It is not our feelings who determine our thoughts, but our thoughts who determine our feelings.
The feelings just follow the thoughts.
God cannot be lied to.
All of us who are unhappy, sad and depressed, are simply full of dark thoughts, and the dark feelings follow.
***
The fear of God is the beginning of wisdom,

the love of God it is the completeness of wisdom.
***
The definition the holiness: sincerity.

The definition of deceitfulness: perversity.
***
Our distrust in God's Love offends Him more than some sins we have committed.
***
The difference between heaven and hell is just a thought.

The thoughts will save us because the thoughts also killed us.

***

God loves you.

God defended the victims from the beginning.
***

The ones who cannot understand the love of God prove that they have never really loved, anybody.

And the sincere love cannot be taught in a book or by words, it is a choice we make.
***

With the feet on the ground and the soul in the sky, you are invincible, the Holy Love of God is all-powerful.
Stay in His Love.
***

"Anything is possible to those who believe" Jesus Christ
***

For the ones that are clean, everything is clean

But for the ones that are dirty everything is dirty, even their minds, their thoughts.

Apostle Paul (Titus 1:15)
***

Think outside the box and you will find God.
You cannot put God the infinite in a Box.
Only with your reason, you can understand the infinite Universe the Eternal God. The box is the Dogma.

The Dogma is created by the ones who want to control you, your mind, and your actions and say that if you have questions ONLY they have the answers.

Do you recognize this pattern?
God gave us the reason.
IT IS OK TO QUESTION THE UNIVERSE.

It is not ok to believe in blasphemous answers.

By this you shall know the Truth: The Truth never blasphemes God!
***

THINKING IT IS NOT ONLY ALOUD
BUT MANDATORY TO FIND THE LIGHT AND TO STAY IN THE LIGHT.
The sleep of reason produces monsters.
***

The sword of the warrior of light it is the word of GOD.
***

God Never left Jesus,
We are the ones who left Jesus and God.
***

The love of God, it is like the sunshine:
The majority cannot feel it because they are just flowers who are too young,
Or they are too old...already dead spiritually.
***

We are not bad robots created by God.
But good children who went bad.
***

We shall never forget that priests and the intellectuals crucified God, and they still do.
***

I must stay above the clouds, in the highest,

where the sky is always blue and where all they say is true.
***

The true human nature and the true Divine Nature:

In a world of blind can be empirically considered that the light does not exist.

But I know it exists, and what the light showed me is the true face of man and God.

The man is full of darkness, and we should beware of darkness because it hides beasts.

And God is light, and His face is Jesus Christ.
***

The testimony of the blind healed by Jesus:

"That is remarkable indeed!" the man said. "You do not know where He is from, and yet He opened my eyes. We know that God does not listen to sinners, but He does listen to the one who worships Him and does His will. Never before has anyone heard of opening the eyes of a man born blind. If this man were not from God, He could not do anything like this." John 9:30
***

"For judgment, I have come into this world, so that the blind may see and those who see may become blind" Jesus Christ
***

The sky is the same everywhere and for everybody!
***

We prove that we love God if we receive His Holy Love.

***

The most important pray is Thanksgiving.

Every day you must say: Thank you God for the sunshine of this day.

When you think you have nothing, thank God that you are alive, that He created you and you will realize that you have everything, because you have the Holy Spirit of God.

Offend not His Spirit.

The ungratefulness creates the internal hell.

The hell or the paradise there are just states of mind created by our thoughts. Think with the thoughts of God.

We have the thoughts of Jesus, who is the true face of God.

***

To know God, you must first know yourself.

You must have an Absolute sincerity with yourself, to know the Absolute in Truth.

***

HAS NO IMPORTANCE WHAT YOU THINK ABOUT ME,

BUT IT IS OF THE HIGHEST IMPORTANCE WHAT WE THINK ABOUT GOD.

AND THIS IS OUR JUDGEMENT.

***

God loves the Human Species, but the Human Species hates God, because the Human Species hates the Truth, and crucifies God every day in the mind.

LOVE GOD WITH YOUR ENTIRE MIND.
Jesus was crucified in a place called Golgotha (the place of the
Head)
***

The root of evil is the mediocrity.

The Nostalgia of sin felt sometimes by the angels and always by the mediocrity.

The sin is followed and preceded by the pathological arrogance of darkness, which hides the mediocrity.
***

A blind man has the liberty to deny the existence of the Sun, but the blind man exists because of the Sun.
God's Advocate.
***

To defeat reality, we must have a Real Faith, not a hypocrite one.
Because God separated from the beginning the light from the darkness.
The Truth from the lie.
***

There are thoughts that kill and thoughts of light that bring life. The thoughts of God are life and light and there were untainted spoken through Jesus Christ.
***

How morally superior the Human Species believes it is to God and His Angels of pure light...

The Human Species believes that it is a victim of God and falsely believes also that is superior to the morality of Jesus Christ, who is the morality of God.

For this arrogance reaps the well-deserved fruits.
***

God is more real that we are.
***

The Truth is that God is love, and the love of God is our judge. And if the infinite love of God decided not to protect some of us in the day of the judgment, how big can be their sins?

An Abyss of sins...

Be good my brothers!
***

Trial and error.

If we do not recognize our errors, we shall forever fail.

The key to success is to see and correct our errors.
***

All those who despise the morality of forgiveness will be saturated by the justice!
***

How morally superior the Human Species thinks it is to ...God... Because it despises the Morality of Christ and believes it is a victim of God.

We shall never forget that priests (Pharisees) and the intellectuals (scribes) crucified God.

The most dangerous soul in hell is the one who believes he is an angel, who has forgotten he has fallen.

And this spirit is the spirit of man.
***

The man's fission from God it is more dangerous and with greater consequences than the fission of matter.

When the soul leaves The Holy Spirit, not only loses the happiness and the spiritual sight, but also the protection of the Spirit of the Truth.

And the Holy Spirit will not tolerate being offended.

Don't find excuses, they are not accepted in front of the Spirit of the Truth.

The Spirit of the Truth defends not the Spirits of Deceit.

God opposes deception,

and all that are born of Him and love the light oppose deception also.
And God is light.

DEUS EST LUX.
***

We are living in the light, but we have our eyes closed.
In a world of blind men, can be empirically considered that the light doesn't exist.
But I know it exists, and what the light showed me is the true face of man and God. The man is full of darkness, and we should beware of darkness because it hides beasts. And God is light, and His face is Jesus Christ.
***

I found Jesus because I made a sacrifice, I sacrificed myself.

***

The definition of Naivety: to trust the love of men and to distrust the love of God.

The Naivety is a Sin Against the Spirit of Truth, and it has the same root as the self- deception.

God and His Holy Angels, oppose deception and self-deception.

***

Only the small people cannot forgive small mistakes.

***

I am not Naïve to Believe in the Love of God but I would be very naïve to believe in the love of men.

***

I forgive you in the Name of Jesus Christ, and I let the Holy Spirit judge us all!

When the truth is too holy to be said, you must let the reality judge the liars.

***

The great journeys are made with small steps, to the highest mountain or the deepest valley.

See reversed Milgram's Paradigm to teach your children to be good men.

***

You cannot crucify and worship God at the same time.

We crucify God by our every mistake.

It is in our power not to make any mistake.

***

"But if you do not forgive, neither will your Father who is in heaven forgive your transgressions." Mark 11:26

The victims from today are yesterday's aggressors, and the victims from the beginning were defended by God.

God loves us because we were born, and we were all born of Him. And the Love of God is our Judge.

***

Return to your first Love, The Holy Spirit.

Because He loves you with true love.

Be not deceived by the lying love of this world because it is a mixture of hate, poison, killer thoughts, and it is just a surrogate, a perverted energy created by the perverted minds that want only to control you like a mechanical animal, and it can only do that if it turns you against God.

Return to your first love, the pure, true love of Paradise, that it is like the sunshine of a pure calm day of spring, and it smells like the most beautiful flowers bathed in the Light.

***

God loves you,

Be not an unfaithful soul.

Return to Him and He will forgive your unfaithfulness, Because

He loves you because you were born,

And you were born of Him.

***

THE NAIVETY IS A GREAT SIN,

BECAUSE THAT MEANS THAT OUR EYES ARE ALREADY BLIND, by our own lack of exterior and interior sincerity.

The naivety is the effect of our spiritual blindness and our spiritual blindness comes from the fear of the truth that says that we made mistakes.

THE BLINDNESS IS DIRECTLY PROPORTIONAL
WITH THE GRAVITY OF OUR MISTAKES.
***

"YOU HAVE BEEN WITH ME FROM THE
BEGINNING"
JESUS CHRIST

The victims from today are yesterday's aggressors,
and the victims from The Beginnings were defended by
God.

God loves the Human Species.

The love of God is our Judge.
***

Imitatio Christi, Imitatio Deus est.
The imitation of Christ is the imitation of God.

***

Do not beg from beggars, love or respect.
Just thank God for all.
***

Receive the Spirit of the Truth! Said Jesus to His
disciples. That means that the Human Species has the
liberty not to receive the Spirit of Truth. It is called self-
deception and it is more common than you think.
***

YOU WERE WITH ME FROM THE BEGINNING.
***

I give up the darkness,
But you give your tears to the night...
***

"Jesus told him: Do not be afraid, just believe.'" Mark 5:36

***

GOD IS WITH ME, AND I AM NOT AGAINST HIM.

***

Every sin is blasphemy because it despises the morality of God.

***

Jesus loves you,

Be not an adulterous soul!

***

Dismas, the good thief the key to the return to paradise. He said:

For us is just!

But it is unjust to crucify God.

***

God told me to forgive.

And whoever despises the Words of the Creator of the infinite Universe, no longer belongs, for this pathological arrogance, to the Human Species.

Because it is written: "you hated me for no reason at all", like animals without reason. And it is written also:" do not name unclean, what GOD made clean" with His blood.

God's Advocate.

***

God loves the humankind, but the humankind loves the darkness rather than the light.

The humankind swims in an ocean of fresh water and it complains that dies of thirst.

The humankind looks at the Sun through a stained glass and says that its rays are dirty, but its eyes are dirty with bad thoughts towards God.

Or closes its eyes and says that the Sun doesn't exist, but it exists because of the Sun.

The humankind likes in a perverted way to believe that God hates her, in order to believe it is morally superior to Him and His angels.

This illusion feeds a pathological arrogance, for what the humankind has left the happiness of the paradise.

And the paradise means to really know that God loves you, and this I am trying to teach you.

***

God loves you, be not an adulterous soul! Be faithful to the Truth!

***

"Amen, I say to you that the publicans and the harlots shall go into the kingdom of God before you."

Jesus Christ to the priests(Pharisees) and intellectuals(scribes), because they believed themselves without mistake.

Jesus loves you, stop despising His love, stop the pathological arrogance of believing that you are morally superior to Him,

because He is the real morality of God, The morality of the Absolute.

***

The Love of God is an infinite ocean, but some hearts are like stones, they will fall into the abyss if they will remain stoned in fear, hate, and lie.

***

In God we trust.

Only in God.

***

Imitatio Christi, imitatio Deus est.

The imitation of Christ, it is the imitation of GOD.

***

Only God is good in an Absolute way.

Even His angels aren't without mistake in front of Him.

To consider yourself without sin it is to make God a liar (Gen 1, 1John 1:10)

Only if we see our mistakes we can correct them.

***

Who says he made no sin makes God a liar. (1John 1:10).

And who is without sin may cast the first stone! (John 8:7).

But are so many that cast out stones ...that means that are so many that believe them self without sin...

***

The greatest sin it is to think you have no sin.

***

"Who is without sin, may throw the first stone." Jesus Christ

***

A reminder for our prayers:

We do not need to remind God to be merciful: He is, He was and He will always be merciful. We must remind ourselves to be merciful, and to forgive our enemies, to receive the mercy of God, and to be forgiven. It is mandatory to forgive If you want to be forgiven.

God is Truth and in Him, it is no lie at all, so if we want to have a good relationship with God, we must begin by being truthful with Him.

69

The hypocrites are the sons of darkness, and from the beginning, God separated the darkness from the light. The original sin of humanity is to believe the lie that it is morally superior to God, that its morality is superior and that it is a victim of God.

The morality of God is the morality of Christ and it is a historical fact that God is our victim. (See The Crucifixion, Jerusalem, Golgotha, Anno Domini 33)
***

If you forgive all, you will be forgiven for all.
***

"Everyone who does evil hates the Light and does not come into the Light for fear that his deeds will be exposed" John 3.20
***

We must not remind God to be Merciful, -----dogma;

but we must remind ourselves that He is Merciful----- real faith;

and we must remind ourselves to be Merciful. ----- good deeds;

God is, was and will always be Merciful. -----real faith.
***

Fear is the mind killer.

Be full of true love through the power of the Cross of God.
***

"For now we see through a glass, darkly; but then face to face: now I know in part; but then shall I know even as also I am known" 1Corinthians 13:12
***

„But wisdom is proved right by all her children" Jesus Christ,

Luke 7:35

***

"I do not fear God, but His absence "Octavian Paler, philosopher.

***

It is written:" For God so loved the world that he gave his one and only Son, that whoever believes in Him shall not perish but have eternal life".

***

Jesus said: the light has come into the world, but people loved darkness rather than the light because their deeds were evil.

***

"God separated from the beginning the darkness from the light." Genesis 1:4

"The light shines into the darkness and the darkness never put it out." John 1:4. Be light!

***

The justice and the mercy of God do not contradict themselves:

"Blessed are they who show mercy, for mercies will be upon them. ,, Matthew 5:7

"For if you forgive the children of men their faults, your Father who is in Heaven will also forgive you your faults ,, Matthew 6:14

"Then the master called him and declared, 'You wicked servant! I forgave all your debt because you begged me. Should you not have had mercy on your fellow servant, just as I had on you?" Mat 18:22

***

The best antidote against a lie is the truth.

71

***

"I want to know God's thoughts; the rest are details."
Albert
Einstein
***

If I can accept the fact that I deserve my pain, why
can't you?
***

"But I say to you that I shall not drink again from this
fruit of the vine until the day in which I shall drink it
with you knew in the Kingdom of my Father." Jesus
Christ.
***

"Fear not, just believe!" Jesus Christ.
***

"Where is your Faith?" Jesus Christ.
***

-What origin are you?
-I am of divine origin.
-What origin are you?
I tell you: THE SKY IS THE SAME EVERYWHERE
and for everybody.
***

A house divided cannot stand.
***

Jesus explained many times that we should forgive to
be forgiven; we should be merciful in order to receive
mercy.

But it seems that not many people understand that
because in their prayers all try to remind God to be good,
but they all forget to remind themselves to be good.

Don't worry, God is good and He did not forget to be
good.

We must repent, forgive and have mercy even on our enemies, because God loves also His enemies, and if you doubt His love or justice that means you know who His enemy is.

***

Do not be naïve, because beautiful words can hide dark thoughts, but the beautiful thoughts give beautiful feelings.

We know the trees by their fruits.

Do not eat from the trees of the knowledge of good and evil, because you will surely die.

Do not believe the blasphemies against God because you will become also a blasphemer!

***

You must clean yourself from the lies of this world, and clean yourself with the Truth, and the truth is the word of God.

***

A madman who looks at the sun through a stained glass can say that the rays of the sun are dirty, but the madman exists because of the sun, and his eyes are dirty.

We all live in paradise but our eyes are dirty with dark thoughts. Clean yourself from the dark thoughts by informational fasting and with The Word of God.

***

Again, a voice came to him a second time, "What God has cleansed, no longer consider unholy „Acts 10:15

We should not name unclean, what God cleansed with His divine blood.

***

"Sanctify them by the truth, your word is truth." John 17: 17

***

"Outside are all who love and make deception."
Revelation 22:15

***

"But the Advocate, the Holy Spirit, whom the Father will send in my name, will teach you all things and will remind you of everything I have said to you." John 14:26

***

He said to him, "Why do you call me good? No one is good but one, that is, God. But if you want to enter into life, keep the commandments."

If Jesus had so much humility not to consider himself perfect in goodness and to give this glory only to God, why do you consider yourselves good?

If I stay in God's commandments, I become truly independent from this fallen world.

***

"Those who exalt themselves will be humbled, and those who humble themselves will be exalted."

***

For this is My blood of the covenant, which is poured out for many for the forgiveness of sins.

Matthew 26:28

***

I will think with the thoughts of God and do God's Moral.

"Now this is eternal life: that they know you, the only true God, and Jesus Christ, whom you have sent." John 17:3.

***

God never left us.

We left Him and unjustly crucified Him.

And he continues to love us, even on the Cross.

But if you want His protection you must descend God from the Cross and say you're sorry for your arrogance of believing that you are morally superior to Him.

God's morality is better, and God's morality is Jesus's morality.

Despise not Jesus, because if you despise Jesus you despise God.

***

The "day of judgment" is to today, and was yesterday. The judgment is individual, not global.

***

The men fear death because they fear God, and they fear God because He shows our true faces because God tells always the truth.

The men fear death because they fear their own reflection in the light of God. The men fear themselves.

***

-Who is God's Advocate?

-The Holy Spirit, Jesus Christ, and any soul that defends the honor of God on this world that has a mad collective consciousness that doubts the love of God.

***

"For he that shall be ashamed of me and of my words, in this adulterous and sinful generation: the Son of man also will be ashamed of him, when he shall come in the glory of his Father with the holy angels. " Marc 8:38

***

"The light of thy body is thy eye. If thy eye be good, thy whole body shall be lightsome. "Mat. 6: 22

***

Not every sinner that knows he's evil will be freed.

Only the sinner that forgave those who sinned against him, and who truly repented.

75

God will know if you truly forgave or if you truly are sorry.

God cannot be lied to.

Jesus said: not everyone who says Lord, Lord, will enter the kingdom of Heaven.

The provocateurs have no power if you do not let yourself provoked if you react in an unpredictable way.

THIS IS THE POWER OF FORGIVENESS.

***

If we forgive we will be forgiven and liberated from the prison of our sins, our "karma".

And then we will be protected like the angels from heaven, like the true victims from The Beginning who didn't rebel against our Heavenly Father. And, if you want to understand, and I pray that you understand, this is the reason that the forgiveness is the absolute power because if we cleaned our sins we are protected by the Holy Spirit.

Be Holy, that means be truthful with yourself, God and the men.

***

Even when I walk through the darkest valley,

I fear no evil,

For God is with me, and I am not against Him.

God's Advocate.

Love God with all your mind.

***

If you want to stay in eternal life stay in His commands.

***

There are many messengers but the Truth is One, that the real Face of God is Jesus Christ.

God is a Good God.

The man is a liar and a murderer (hater) from the beginning.

The men are the aggressors from the beginning.
***

The fruit of the tree of good and evil, it is the lie that we are morally superior to God.
***

Do not deceive yourself, God cannot be lied to.

Whatever a man sows, he will reap in return.

The one who sows to please his flesh, from the flesh will reap destruction, but the one who sows to please the Spirit, from the
Spirit he will reap eternal life." Apostle Paul

In order to reap: the forgiveness from God, and consequently His Protection,

We must sow:

Repentance

The forgiveness of ALL that trespassed against us.

The mercy of ALL who need our mercy.

In our prayers, we must stop reminding God to be good, He is good, He is better than some of us will ever want to know, He is Absolute in Good, Beauty and Truth. By begging His Mercy, we offend Him. He is already Absolute and Infinite in Mercy. There is no higher value than the infinite.

What it is good to do it is to articulate our Faith in His Infinite
Goodness, THE REAL TRUST IN HIS HOLY LOVE.

This is the definition of Faith: to know that Only God is Good and the Human Species is evil because it has chosen to be evil.

At the beginning, God created the Humankind good, after His image, but the Humanity desecrated His Image, and the True Image of God is Jesus Christ.

In our prayers, we must remember ourselves to be good, to be merciful and to really forgive and love one another.

Only in this way, we will receive His Mercy, His Forgiveness and His Holy Infinite Love.

Remember His Words:

Forgive our mistakes in the same way we forgive those who have made mistakes against us. (Lord's Prayer).

Blessed are the merciful because they will receive Mercy.

And if you still think that God will forgive an unforgiving soul, or have mercy on the merciless remember the words of Jesus:"

IF YOU DO NOT FORGIVE NEITHER YOUR FATHER WHO IS IN HEAVEN WILL FORGIVE YOU" Mark 11:26

If you give others: mercy, forgiveness, and sincere, holy love: You will receive from God ten times more in return.

But if you beg God, to forgive you, or have mercy on you, and you persist in hate, unforgiveness and lack of mercy, you should know that you beg in vain, and you will only succeed to fool yourself and maybe others, that you are forgiven, but YOU WILL NOT BE ABLE TO FOOL GOD.

***

The love of God is our judge and savior at the same time.

THE SKY IS THE SAME EVERYWHERE AND OVER ALL.

Over cities and villages, over powerful countries and third world countries, over angels and men, over the good and evil ones.

Our facts return to us.

If we forgive and repent, God is merciful and will return our innocence to us, as we were IN THE BEGINNING.

THE LOVE OF GOD IS OUR JUDGE AND SAVIOR.
***

We shall think only the thoughts of Jesus, the thoughts of God, and the word of God will make us clean, and free because the word of God is the truth.
***

"Above the clouds, the sky is always blue." Saint Therese de Lisieux
***

This book is written for the ones who search God. Not for the ones who search the darkness, to hide their sins from themselves.
***

Fear is the very nature of darkness.
***

FEAR NOT, JUST BELIEVE! Marc. 5:36
***

The love of God is our judge, and if the infinite love of God, decided to severely punish some of us, how big can be their sins ...An Abyss of sins...
***

And behold I am with you all days, even to the consummation of the world. Mat. 28:20

***

Because you say it is hard to forgive: you prove that only the strong can forgive.

Forgiveness is the power absolute!

If you forgive, you will be forgiven by God, and if you are forgiven for all you will be protected like the victims from The Beginning. You will probably say: what is to forgive, we believe that we are innocent.

Well, you can believe whatever you choose.

But just remember: what we believe about God, judge us. And the love of God is our judge.

***

The love of God is Just.

And I just need the love of God.

***

When we blame others for our mistakes, we give them our power.

We are self-determined, and therefore responsible.

We are free and therefore responsible.

If we see our mistakes, we can correct them.

If we blame others, that means we believe we have no mistakes.

***

The sin against the Holy Spirit will not be forgiven.

If you say that the light is darkness and the darkness light, it is an unforgivable sin." We know that God is light, and in Him is no darkness at all".(John1:5).

***

You must forgive to be forgiven,

You must love to receive God's love.

***

We function by the algorithm of trial and error.

If we do not recognize our errors, we will forever fail. Be smart, and see your errors.

***

My body is the temple of the Holy Spirit.

***

John spoke of the evil one as the "antichrist".

The ones who disrespect the morality of forgiveness are all antichrists. You must understand that before you can say you are really a Christian.

A true Christian really respects Jesus.

The hypocrisy is a sin against the Holy Spirit, against the spirit of The Science of God, against the Spirit of the Truth.

***

For The infinite love of God, the pain that this rebelled species produces is nothing, is like a child would throw a hand of sand in the ocean, the ocean wouldn't be troubled by it. In the same way with the cross. God can carry our cross because He really loves us, and He loves us because we were born, and we were born of God.

GOD IS AN INFINITE OCEAN OF PURE, TRUE, HOLY LOVE.

If we want to be sons and daughters of God we must think with the thoughts of God.

We can begin by believing His word. God is not a liar; the human species is.

And God loves the Human Species in truth. Stay in the Truth! Return to the light!

***

Maranatha (Aramaic): Come here Lord Jesus, come here. 1 Cor.16:22

***

81

I LOVE YOU ALL WITH THE LOVE OF CHRIST!

And the love of God, which is in Christ and in me, through the Holy Spirit, is our Judge and Savior at the same time.

***

But you say: What is to forgive? we are good.

In what darkness do you live, I pity you...

When the arrogance is greater than the will to see, only God can save thee.

***

The servants are fearful, but the sons are full of love.

Moses was a servant, Jesus is the Son of God, first of all, sons of God, the highest of the angels, the king of angels, the highest created soul in the hierarchy of Heaven, the closest to God.

And He descended to us, to save us from ourselves.

***

Jesus also said: For what tell you that I am good?

Only God is good. (Mark 10:18)

If Jesus Christ, said that only God is good, in what darkness are the men that believe that they are without mistake, and always others are to blame.

***

JESUS, THE SON OF GOD, I TRUST IN YOU!

The Son loves us with the love of the Father, and the true face of God is Jesus Christ.

John said:" the perfect love cast out fear."

The one who is perfect in the love for God is made perfect by God.

Adam and Eve knew that God exists.

And they now have forgotten.

They not only forgotten about God, but about who they really are, and now they believe that they are just evolved animals. They are not evolved animals, but they are decayed men, they are devolved men. This is the theory of Human Devolution.

And the real face of the man is the Son of Man, Jesus Christ.

Ecce Homo, Behold the Man, said Pilate, without knowing what profound truth he said.

Adam and Eve, are the metaphoric representation of the true men from the beginning. We all were Adam or Eve. In the beginning, we were milliards. At the beginning, "a third of stars fall from the sky". Revelation 12:4.

Knowing or believing in the existence of God it is not sufficient to enter paradise.

To return to the light you must first open your eyes, you must see yourself in the Mirror of the Holy Spirit, you must see your mistakes, you must be sorry for your mistakes(repent) and you must forgive if you want to be forgiven , and be cleansed in the blood of Jesus Christ, the beloved Son of God, and only than you can enter the lost Paradise.

   ***

In reality, the darkness fears the light.

   ***

Do not name unclean what God cleansed.
***

Do not be naïve because:

The beautiful words can hide dark thoughts but beautiful thoughts give beautiful feelings.

The Holy Spirit inspired me because I despised the perversity of the lie.
***

GOD LOVES YOU BECAUSE YOU WERE BORN
GOD DEFENDED THE VICTIMS FROM THE BEGINNING.

If you forgive, you will be forgiven and logically, protected by God.

If you know that you are in the prison (of sin) justly it is not sufficient to be liberated.

You must first: repent.

And second: forgive all.

And God will know, and He will set you free and He will protect you.
***

It is not sufficient to know that you are in the prison (of sin) justly, to be liberated, but is mandatory.

A real tragedy would be, to be in a prison and to believe that you are free.
***

THANK YOU, GOD, FOR ALL!
AND ABOVE ALL, THANK YOU!

To be always above all, just thank always God.

It is impossible to save someone from himself.
But nothing is impossible to God.
***

The fear of God is the beginning of wisdom.
The love of God is the completeness of wisdom.
***

We must work with and from the honest, holy love of men and not from the fear of the punishment, of failure.
***

The thoughts will save us, in the same way, the thoughts killed us.
***

Cleanse me, My God!
Above the dark clouds of fear, distrust, and pride, the sky is always blue.
***

The Thoughts of Light are thoughts of God.
We think 30 000 thoughts daily.
The quality of our thoughts determines the quality of our life.
***

If you think sincerely:
Thank you Lord for the rays of light of this morning, every morning, you will discover that you were already in Paradise, but you were too ungrateful to feel it.
This is what Jesus said on the day of His crucifixion, and He also did not feel the cross as a human would do, because of the power of the true, holy love.
Who really loved, understands.
***

Food is not love and the sex is not love also.
***

"Be merciful, as our Father from Heaven merciful is."
Jesus Christ
***

And Jesus said, "For the judgment of this world I have come, that those who do not see may see and that those who see may become blind."
***

In this world, sometimes the gift is bigger than the heart, but in Heaven, the heart is bigger than the gift.
***

Can a blind lead a blind?
Will not fall both into the abyss?
***

"A city which sits on a mountain cannot be hidden."
***

"HAVE NO FEAR, just believe!"
That God is an infinite ocean of holy love.
***

IT IS THE HOLY LOVE OF GOD THAT JUDGES US.
And if the love of God has found some of us guilty and decided not to protect them in the day of the justice How big must their sins ...
An Abyss of sins ...
***

Jesus is the light of the world
But this world loves the darkness rather than the light.
Because its deeds are evil, and it does not want to see its true face ...
***

Whoever despises the MORALITY OF FORGIVENESS will be saturated by the JUSTICE.
***

It is not important to be rich, but it is very important not to be poor.

***

Who cannot understand the love of God, proves he never really loved, anybody.

***

Deceive not yourselves
God cannot be lied to ...

***

Who does not respect the truth, respects not God, because God is the Truth.

***

It is the love of God that judges us

***

God loves you,
But you are an adulterous soul, that left the Spirit of Truth for an arrogant illusion. Be faithful to the Truth.

***

CONSIDER NOT UNCLEAN, WHAT GOD MADE CLEAN, WITH HIS BLOOD.

***

The love of God is our judge.
We have the Karma we deserve.

***

God is Human.
This Species became posthuman.

***

I am God's Advocate on this prison planet.
Not that God needs protection, but I need His protection.
Anybody who offends God offends me also.

***

Trial and error.

We function by the algorithm of Trial and Error, if we do not recognize our errors we become dysfunctional.
***

To be politically incorrect can bring you into paradise.
***

Who is so low, to think that God lies, does not deserve the paradise.
***

God loves the Human Species, but the Human Species crucifies God every day in its collective consciousness.
LOVE GOD WITH YOUR ENTIRE MIND.
Jesus was crucified in a place called Golgotha (the place of the Head).
***

"The truth will make you free. "Jesus Christ.
***

Jesus Christ is the light of the world, and whoever walks with Him, will never walk in darkness.
But we know, because He told us, that this world loves darkness rather than the light because its deeds are evil.
***

To control your life, your destiny you must first control yourself.
***

The victimization is self-deception, a perversity of the soul, an imbecility.
***

The one who denies the existence of the light it is a volunteer blind.
Because doesn't want to see his true face and the true face of God.
And the true face of God is Jesus Christ.
***

To control the world, you must first control yourself.
***

The heart has its reasons, that the reason does not understand..."
Descartes
***

And Avraham said:
If they did not listen to Moses and the prophets
Will not believe even someone will rise from the dead.
***

Sin against the Holy Spirit: to call the darkness light, and light darkness.
Unforgivable=any punishment is allowed for this.
***

Clean me, God, with the truth, your word is the truth.
***

If you will sincerely say: thank you God for the light of this day, and you will enter paradise, where you are protected by God.
Divide not, and be not divided against God!
***

You cannot be happy because you are naïve, to trust this world and to distrust God.

In God, we trust, only in God, and those in whom God lives, and it is not crucified.
***

Be rich in good deeds, words, and thoughts and you shall never fear the light, and you shall never hide in the shadow of the lying trees.
We are all naked of secrets in front of God.
The unfaithfulness is a sin against the Holy Spirit.
***

TO ADMIT YOUR MISTAKES, IT IS TO RECOGNIZE YOUR POWER!

***

The men self-destroy with their own sins.

KARMA all Buddhists know it is real.

The human species programs its future, in the present by doing good or evil, thinking good or evil, speaking good or evil.

The nostalgia of sin felt sometimes by the angels and always by the mediocre.

We are responsible for our own mistakes, and we are responsible for our lives, therefore we are powerful, we are masters of our Karma, destiny.

TO ADMIT YOUR MISTAKES, IT IS TO RECOGNIZE YOUR POWER!

God loves us.

In the same way, somebody despised your love, in the same way, you despise the love of God.

Believe not that you are morally superior to God!

Believe not that you are a victim of God!

Believe not that your morality is superior to the morality of the Cross, to the morality of Christ.

Because the morality of Christ is the morality of God, and it is a historical fact that God is our victim.

***

We sin because of our mediocrity in good deeds, the self-deception that follows the sin, builds a pathological arrogance.

***

Who believes not God, makes Him a liar. In God, we trust. Only in God.

***

THE LIGHT CAME INTO THE WORLD AND THIS WORLD LOVED THE DARKNESS RATHER THAN THE LIGHT.

***

This world is a forest of trees of good and evil that make fruits full of poison.

Christ is the tree of life.

Feed upon His Words!

***

Jesus is the light of this world.

Call the light and darkness will flee.

***

Can a blind lead a blind?

***

Anyone who offends God will spend a holiday in the hell of their own minds. Unforgettable holiday.

Make your holidays holy.

If you make your every day holy you will have a holiday for eternity.

***

How could Jesus support the Cross?

He is God.

By the Power of the Honest, Holy Love.

***

The word of God makes us clean.

***

I must convince my brothers to Trust in Jesus if they want to get out of hell. To trust the Power of Light.

***

I am an old Atlantean, an ancient awakened.

I must not repeat the mistakes of the past.

***

Who deserves to be defended, will be defended by God.
***

My Faith saved me.

If I am politically correct, I only have a temporary advantage, if I am divinely correct I will have peace for eternity.
***

I will always respect the morality of Jesus Christ.
***

The man created a web of lies, in which everybody loves to believe. By the way, every prisoner thinks his not guilty.

The real war it is not against the matter but against the multitude of thoughts of the sinners who adore thinking they are clean.
***

"There will be wars and rumors of wars." Jesus Christ.
***

To know God, you must first know yourself.

You must have an Absolute sincerity with yourself to know the Absolute.
***

In a world of blind men, it can be empirically considered that the light does not exist.
***

"I tell the Truth, this is why you do not believe me "Jesus
***

And I walked in paradise and I saw a rose surrounded by weed. The next time I would like to see a field of roses surrounding a weed.
***

Do you want the truth?

You can't handle the truth.

God is real, and Jesus is my savior.

I hope we will meet all in the light of God.

I will teach you the path to the light.

God is Just.

Buddha is also right, reincarnation is also real.

We deserve our suffering because we were and are evil.

What is politically correct can be morally wrong.

War is evil, greed is evil, denying the existence of God is evil,

Believing the dark philosophy was the original sin.

***

"The light has come into the world, but the people loved the darkness more than the light because their deeds were evil" Jesus Christ.

***

Beware of the love of men and the fury of the angels,

Because the men know not how to love, and when they love, they love towards death, and the angels know not how to hate, and when they hate they hate to death.

***

God is a good God

He will forgive us if we really want to come back to Him. God is love, and Jesus is the evidence of His deep love for the humankind.

We crucify Him every day in our minds and in our hearts, but He loves us.

***

I walk with God.

***

"Where is your heart, there is your treasure." Jesus Christ.

***

Who am I?

An aggressor from The Beginnings who repented and forgave and was saved.

Who are you?

Also, aggressors from The Beginnings who think they are victims.

***

"Who came from God listens to His Words."

"I tell you the truth: before Avraham, I am." Jesus

***

"When I am in the world I am the light of the world." Jesus.

***

Jesus is a victim from The Beginning who was protected by God at the beginning, at the time of the rebellion.

With the crucifixion, He demonstrated the Power of the Love of God and He revealed to us the True Face of God.

***

The word of God defeats the lie of the beasts.

***

"If you obey my teaching you are really my disciples, you will know the truth

and the truth will make you free." Jesus

***

"The Father will give you everything that you will ask In My Name, ask and you will receive so that your happiness will be complete "Jesus Christ.

***

"If the world hates you, remember it has hated Me first." GOD, the Holy Bible.

***

"Who hates me, hates my Father also." Jesus Christ
***

For some of us does not matter that they die in stupid wars, but more importantly, it is to die with a full belly.
***

Clean me with the truth Your word is the truth.
***

We must be light in order to stay in the light.
***

God's Advocate:

Jesus loves you but you are an adulterous soul.

Jesus loves you but you despise His love.

Jesus loves you but you are an unfaithful soul.
***

May the power of the light of Jesus Christ give you spiritual Power, Light, and true Love.
***

I shell carry my cross every day with a smile on my face, through the power of true love.
***

I love you all with the love of Jesus and the love of God, who is in Jesus, is our judge.
***

The most important prayer is Thanksgiving.

Every day you must say:
Thank you, God, for the sunshine of this day.

When you think you have nothing, thank God that you are alive, that He created you and you will realize that

you have everything, because you have the Holy Spirit of God.
Offend not His Spirit.

The ungratefulness creates the internal hell.

The hell or the paradise are just states of mind created by our thoughts.
Think with the thoughts of God.

We have the thoughts of Jesus,
 who is The True Image of The One True God.
***
Beware of the darkness because it hides beasts.
***
The patience and goodness of God
Tells us to repent from our mistakes.
***
Trial and error.
We must see our errors, to be a good Natural Intelligence (see A.I.)
***
We are living in the light, but we have our eyes closed.
***
"Glory to God in the highest! "Archangel Gabriel
***
The sword of the Truth, the shield of faith.
***
But know I live in a world, where the hate of God is infiltrated within ordinary people, apparently "innocent", which when I talk about God, they attack with blasphemies.
This represents the banality of evil.
***

Jesus loves you but you are an adulterous soul.
***

The Nostalgia of sin felt sometimes by the angels,

and always by the mediocrity.
***

"At the beginning, the word already existed."
***

Who doesn't believe that God is Good, offends Him, actually makes an unpardonable sin.
***

We offend God when we doubt His Goodness. The disbelief is the disrespect of God, and this a sin against the Holy Spirit.
***

"You are clean because of the Word I have said." Jesus
***

If you believe that you are good and innocent, that means logically that you believe that God is not.
***

I prefer to think that God is right and all Humankind is wrong.
***

"To who loved a lot, a lot will be forgiven "Luke 7:47
***

"Your faith saved you!" Jesus Christ
***

Jesus saves.
***

God loves you!
But you are an adulterous soul.
***

Do not be fooled to be turned against God, you will lose your Protector.

Be always advocates of God to be protected by the Advocate of God (the Holy Spirit).

Be one with the advocate of God, with the Spirit of the Truth, who protects the truth, not the deception.

Be full of truth.

The Spirit of Truth opposes deception.

***

"Where is your heart, there is your treasure." Jesus Christ.

***

May the Power of Love of Jesus Christ, give you happiness and light.

May the Power of Light of Jesus Christ, give you wisdom and love.

***

God's Advocate:

I defend the honor, dignity of God, in this world, even with the price of offending this world.

I oppose deception.

***

Philosophy teaches you how to think.

I teach the philosophy of the light.

***

"Sanctify them by the truth, your word is the truth. "John 17:17

***

-The Humankind believes the lie, that it is a victim of God, so morally superior to Him.

Can you blame the Human species of naivety?

-No, but of BAD-WILL

***

The thoughts will save us because the thoughts also killed us.

***

The Philosophy of darkness is more dangerous than the atomic bomb because it separates us from our protector, God.

***

The wonder exists in front of you
The universe and we are the wonders.

***

Socrates said: "Know yourself"
God said, "you shall know the Truth and the Truth will make you free."
So, the conclusion: if you truly know yourself, God will make you free.

***

This sinful and unfaithful generation demands a sign but only the Sign of the Cross will be given.

***

If I doubt you, you are offended.
Why should God be not offended?

***

A HOUSE DIVIDED CANNOT STAND,
If you are divided against God you will be cast out.
We must be all GOD'S ADVOCATES in order to FIGHT the ones who try to divide us against God.

***

Do not be fools, the Sin Against the Holy Ghost will never be forgiven
Respect God with all your mind, and you will enter in paradise.

***

I cannot heal you, but I know someone who can.
Jesus, I call you,
Jesus, I call your Holy Spirit
Your Holy Spirit really loves us!

In the Name of Jesus Christ of Nazareth, Open your eyes, my brother!

***

The truth is the word of God. The logos, the law of nature. The word of Christ is also the word of God.

If the laws of nature make the planets spin around the sun, The word of Christ has the same power.

***

I want to know the thoughts of God...Einstein said... But we have the thoughts of Christ, who is The True Image Of The One True God.

***

Christmas doesn't mean cakes but the love of God.

Receive Him!

Despise Not God!

***

We wake up only to continue to dream, a nightmare that we like.

We love God when we accept and recognize His Holy Love.

***

"I am the light of the world, who walks with me, will never walk in darkness." Jesus Christ

***

God will never leave me.

***

The Human Species has become a post-human species.

Because it despised the Love, The Truth and The Path of God. But they choose the hate, the self-deception, and the wandering.

***

Have you ever felt the Nobility of a soul who did not leave God, that Nobility of a character of divine morality, a divine soul that lives in the light, and didn't made so much evil to hide at the shadow of the lying trees.

I felt.

I've seen.

I was.

***

"In love, there is no fear, the perfect love cast out fear." 1 John 4:18.

***

Who doesn't believe God, makes Him a liar.

***

Trial and error: algorithm
If you see not your error
Then infinite Trial.

***

"For us is just, because we receive the punishment for our sins but God is not guilty. „ The good thief on the cross, and after this thought He was accepted back in Paradise.

***

It is not your business to condemn their hearts, but of the Holy Spirit.

***

I love you with the love of God.

***

I am demonstrating logically not only the justice but also the infinite Love of God.

***

I love you with the love of the Holy Spirit, given to me by God. I respect and protect the Holy Spirit and he protects me.

Were a team, and I am for eternity His Advocate.
***

Return to your first love.
The Spirit of Truth and of the True Love, The Holy Love Of God.
***

"Who hates Me, hates My Father also." Jesus Christ.
***

"Be merciful, as your Father in heaven, merciful is." Jesus Christ.
***

The battle is of the thoughts!
The war is psychological.
***

"If a blind leads a blind, they will both fall into Abyss." Mat.15: 14
***

"We know the trees by their fruits." Mat. 7: 20.
***

"I am the truth, the path, and the life." Jesus Christ.
***

"A castle which stays on a mountain cannot be hidden.
You, my disciples, are the light of the world." Mat. 5: 14.
***

"I am the Light of the World.
Whoever walks with me, will never walk in darkness." John 8:12.
***

-How can I stay in the light?
- "If you want to stay in the eternal life stay in His commandments." Mat .19 :17
***

God cannot be lied to.

***

Every war is a racist war; its foundation is the illusion of a born superiority of a group.
***

I tell the truth, that's why you do not believe me.
***

We are programming or future now, by doing good or evil, by speaking good or evil, by thinking good or evil.
***

Who denies the light, is a volunteer blind.
***

"You have been with Me from the beginning." Jesus Christ.
***

"If the world hates you, just remember it has hated Me first." God, The Holy Bible.
***

God knows our hearts.
The love of God is just, and I just need the love of God.
***

I have no fear because God is with me, and I am not against Him.
***

The ones who do not want to listen to God, are the ones who do not want to see their mistakes because God tells always the truth.
***

The ones who do not want to know God are the ones who do not want to know their sins.
***

"Perfect love, cast out fear."1 John 4:18.
***

"Not only with bread feeds a man, but with any word that comes out of God. ,,Mat. 4:4

***

The opposite of love it is not hate but fear.
***

In a world of blind men, can be empirically considered that the light doesn't exist.

But I know it exists, and what the light showed me is the true face of man and God.

The man is full of darkness, and we should beware of darkness because it hides beasts.

And God is light, and His face is Jesus Christ.
***

"God is always with me because I always do what pleases Him." Jesus Christ.
***

Dress the coat of goodness, of light, of the sincere love, of the Holy Love;

The light shines into the darkness and the darkness never put it out.
***

The rejection of fear.

We must have God's perspective,

In the same way, Moses climb the dark cloud, in the same way, we should give up the frightened and desperate perspective of this world.

Above the clouds, the sky is always blue.

The blue sky is the word and the hope of God.

The dark clouds are our illusions.

Respect God's word.
***

We must think with thoughts of light and the thoughts of light are the thoughts of God.

Despise not His Word!
***

We shall never forget that priests and the intellectuals crucified God.

***

We must think with the thoughts of God.

Despise not His Word.

***

And the Spirit and I say: come here, Lord Jesus come here!

You are the same yesterday, today and forever!

***

What God has cleansed, you must not call unclean." Acts 10: 15.

***

"You were made clean by the words of God" Jesus Christ.

***

Keep telling the Name and Rank of our Lord Jesus Christ.

***

The love of God is our Judge.

***

GOD IS WITH ME

And as long I am with God, and not rebel, nobody can touch me!

And why it is of the highest importance to keep the algorithm: God's Advocate.

***

If you forgive all you will be forgiven for all.

***

To be politically incorrect can drive you into Heaven.

***

"For what have you fear? you poor in Faith!" Jesus Christ

The fear is one of the fruits of the arrogance!
We only fear what we consider evil.
And GOD IS GOOD.
***

The philosophy and the Socratic will of self-knowing saved my soul through Jesus Christ.
***

Whoever lives in the lie is the slave of the lie.
***

The sex and death sell the best, and this world loves the darkness rather than the light.
***

For me, God and Jesus Christ, are more real than you are.
***

"Great thing it is to fall into the hands of the living God." Peter.
***

Any soul that doesn't receive, but despises the Holy Love of God is an adulterous soul.
The banality of blasphemy,
The banality of evil it is very dangerous for our souls.
***

"FEAR NOT, JUST BELIEVE!" JESUS CHRIST
***

In comparison with the first civilization from the beginning, this world is a big Babylon zoo.
***

"Where Lord?
Where is the body, there will be the vultures!" Luke 17: 37.
***

The sin of fearing God:

"Fear not, you poor in Faith! "Jesus. Mat 8: 26.

"But the fearful (cowardly) and unbelieving and the abominable and murderers and whoremongers and sorcerers and idolaters and all liars, they shall have their portion in the pool burning with fire and brimstone, which is the second death. "Revelation 21:8.

THE FEAR IS THE VERY NATURE OF DARKNESS.
God's Advocate.
***

The art of true love is the art of true life in the Holy Spirit, it is the eternal life.

And when the Holy Spirit of God is in us, we must let Him love our neighbor with His Holy Love and we must remember that the Holy Love of God is our Judge.
Be Holy, as God is Holy.
The lying love of the perverted spirit it is the greatest enemy of God, and because of that, the perverted spirits were, are and will be severely punished by the Holy Love of God.
***

I know that God exists.
***

The banality of evil it a new concept but an old truth.
***

This world is a forest of trees of good and evil that make fruits that poison us.

Only the word of God is clean and good to eat.

The rest is venom.
***

Jesus said:" I am the light of the world, and whoever walks with me will never walk in darkness". (John 8:12)

I walk with Jesus, and I do not fear His Light, I do not despise His Love, I respect His Morality of Forgiveness, with my entire mind and heart.

The limit of forgiveness is the Sin Against the Holy Spirit. (Mark 3:29, Matthew 12:31)

And without Him I would probably be not alive, because the love of men is full of poison, the science is without holy love, and the morality of men it is no longer humane, but the law of the jungle. And whoever despises the law of God, will become a slave of the law of the jungle.

Jesus saves! Jesus loves you!
To stay in the light means to stay in the Truth.
The Truth is the Word of God.
***

In love, there is no fear and perfect love cast out fear.
Because fear has in it the punishment.

And who fears is not perfect in love and loves not with the perfect love of GOD.

The fear of God is the beginning of wisdom,

The love of God is the completeness of wisdom.

The men like darkness rather than the light because they fear the light.

The fear kills the mind.

We must work with and from the honest love of men and not from the fear of the punishment, of failure.
***

The banality of evil is more dangerous than the obvious evil because we think is innocent.

We are all fallen from God's grace.

Nobody is good, there are no innocents on this Prison Planet. Only when you see the darkness in you and in others can you see the goodness of God. The problem with this species is that it considers itself good. We are not, only GOD is.
***

There are many messengers but the Truth is One.
God is a Good God, and His True Image is Jesus Christ. The man is an aggressor from the beginning.
***

"Whoever hates his brother is a murderer, and you know that no murderer has eternal life abiding in him." 1 John 3:15
***

From the beginning:
God separated the light from the darkness.
Be light!
***

With this book, I don't want to prove to you that I am good,
but that GOD IS GOOD.
***

-What is the truth?
-The truth is the word of God
-And the truth will make us free and clean.
***

"This world will pass, but my words will never pass." Jesus Christ.
***

"If you obey my teachings you are really my disciples,
You will know the truth and the truth will set you free."
***

We are all sons of Cain.

" We indeed justly: for we receive the due reward of our deeds. But this Man (God) hath done no evil.

And he said to Jesus: Lord, remember me when thou shalt come into thy kingdom.

And Jesus said to him: Amen I say to thee: This day thou shalt be with me in paradise. "Luke 23

Whoever shall exalt himself shall be humbled: and he that shall humble himself shall be exalted. Mat.23:12
***

Deceive not yourselves
God cannot be lied to ...
***

"THE COLLECTIVE MADDENS IS CALLED SANITY" P.
Coelho.
It is the love of God that judges us.
***

CONSIDER NOT UNCLEAN, WHAT GOD MADE CLEAN, WITH HIS BLOOD.
***

God is Human.
This Species became posthuman.
***

I am God's Advocate on this prison planet.
Not that God needs protection, but I need His protection. Anybody who offends God offends me also.
***

Trial and error.
We function by the algorithm of Trial an Error, if we do not recognize our errors we become dysfunctional.
***

Thank you, God, for this bread (the word of God) and for these fishes. And they were multiplied...

***

To control the world, you must first control yourself.
***

"The heart has its reasons, that the reason does not understand..." Descartes.
***

And Avraham said:
If they did not listen to Moses and the prophets
Will not believe even someone will rise from the dead."
***

Clean me, God, with the truth, your word is the truth.
***

No matter of the pain, you must say: thank you God for the light of this day, and you will enter paradise, where you are protected by God.

Divide not, and be not divided against God!
***

The unfaithfulness is a sin against the Holy Spirit.
***

The men self-destroy with their own sins.

KARMA all Buddhists know it is real.

The human species programs its future, in the present by doing good or evil, thinking good or evil, speaking good or evil. The nostalgia of sin felt sometimes by the angels and always by the mediocre.

We are responsible for our own mistakes, and we are responsible for our lives, therefore we are powerful, we are masters of our Karma, destiny.

TO ADMIT YOUR MISTAKES, IT IS TO RECOGNIZE YOUR POWER!
***

We sin because of our mediocrity in good deeds, the self-deception which follows the sin, builds a pathological arrogance.

***

Who believes not God, makes Him a liar.
***

THE LIGHT CAME INTO THIS WORLD, AND THIS WORLD LOVED THE DARKNESS RATHER THAN THE LIGHT.

This world is a forest of trees of good and evil that make fruits full of poison. Christ is the tree of life.

Feed upon His Words!
***

Jesus is the light of this world.
Call the light and the darkness will flee.
***

"Can a blind lead a blind?" Jesus Christ.
***

Beware of the priests (Pharisees), for they are hypocrites.
***

Anyone who offends God will spend a holiday in the hell of their own minds. Unforgettable holiday.
***

How could Jesus support the Cross?
He is God.
By the power of the honest, holy love.
The word of God makes you clean.
***

Not everybody has the authority to use the Name of Jesus.
Only believers do.
Not everybody are the believers they say they are.
***

I have to convince my brothers to Trust in Jesus if they want to get out of hell. To trust the Power of Light.
***

Who deserves to be defended, will be defended by God.
***

My Faith saved me.

If I am politically correct, I only have a temporary advantage, if I am divinely correct I will have peace for eternity.
***

Some of us, unfortunately, will never wake up. I have tried to wake them up but they simply don't want to.

They don't want to see their sins, they consider that they are whiter than the Pope, but they are more tainted than the Dalmatians.
***

I will always respect the morality of Jesus Christ.
***

The darkness is the self-deception.

A dark mind wants not the light because wants not to see its mistakes.

Here on this prison planet, Earth, there only a few who truly love God because God says always the Truth.
***

There will be wars and rumors of wars.
***

"The light has come into the world, but the people loved the darkness more than the light because their deeds were evil"

Jesus Christ

The morality of God is the morality of forgiveness.

Jesus has applied the morality of forgiveness and God gave Him the Power of the Holy Spirit, The Power of light, The Absolute Power.
***

Beware of the love of the men and the fury of the angels, because the men know not how to love, and when they love, they love towards death, and the angels know not how to hate, and when they hate, they hate to death.

Examples:

The lying heart, the wickedness, the perverted spirit.

The surrogate of real love.

The greatest sin against the Holy Spirit.

The Blasphemy Against the Holy Spirit shall not be forgiven, not then, not now, not in the future.

See also the psychoanalysis of Sigmund Freud, to understand the mechanism of the dark subconscious, put in motion by the lying hearts of the fallen men from the beginning.

The judgment of Atlantis will repeat itself.

This is a warning and a judgment if the human species repents not from the wickedness of the lying heart.

To be good it is not an option, it is an obligation, for the sake of future generations.

***

Where is your heart, there is your treasure.

***

Who am I?

An aggressor from the beginning who repented and was saved.

Who are you?

Also, aggressors from the beginning who think they are victims.

***

"Who comes from God listens to His Words "Jesus Christ.

***

"If you obey my commandments you will stay in my love, as I obeyed my Father's commandments and I stayed in His love." Jesus

***

For some of us does not matter that they die in stupid wars, but more importantly, it is to die with a full belly.
***

Clean me with the truth, your word is the truth.
***

We must be light in order to stay in the light.
***

May the power of the light of Jesus Christ give you Spiritual power, Light and true Love.
***

I shell carry my cross every day with a smile on my face, through the power of true love.
***

I love you all with the love of Jesus, and the love of God is our judge.
***

We create what our will chooses.
Choose not the darkness, the self-deception. God gives only good gifts.
***

Beware of the darkness because it hides beasts.
***

We must be rich in good deeds!

We are not bad robots created by God.
But good children who went bad.

Our consciousness is not an epiphenomenon.
Our true nature is the Free and Immortal Consciousness.
We are all pieces of God.
God loves us with an infinite love, even when we went bad.

***

Glory to God in the highest.
***

The sword of the Truth.
The shield of faith.
***

What would have I done if I were a soldier in the army of Hitler?
I would have respected the Authority of God even with the price of my life. Why should I make other sins?
***

We offend God when we doubt His Goodness.

The disbelief is the disrespect of God, and this a sin against the Holy Spirit.
***

If you believe that you are good and innocent, that means logically that you believe that God is not.
***

"To who loved a lot, a lot will be forgiven"
***

"Your faith saved you!"
***

Jesus saves.
***

Do not let be fooled to be turned against God You will lose your Protector.
***

"Where is your heart, there is your treasure." Jesus Christ
***

God's Advocate:
I defend the honor, dignity of God, in this world, even with the price of offending this world.

I oppose deception.
***

Do not beg from beggars.
***

Do not be fools, the Sin Against the Holy Ghost will never be forgiven.

Respect God with all your mind, and you will enter in paradise.
***

The truth is the word of God. The logos, the law of nature.

The word of Christ is also the word of God.

If the laws of nature make the planets spin around the sun, the word of Christ has the same power.
***

We love God when we accept and recognize His Holy Love.
***

"The light shines into the darkness, and the darkness never put it out."
***

"Your Faith saved you!"
***

We are programming our future now, by doing good or evil, by speaking good or evil, by thinking good or evil.
***

Whoever denies the light, is a volunteer blind.
***

The opposite of love it is not hate but fear.
***

Trial and error.

If we do not recognize our errors we shall forever fail. The key to success is to see and correct our errors.
***

"For what have you fear, you poor in Faith!" Jesus Christ

The fear is one of the fruits of the arrogance! We only fear what we consider evil.

***

The philosophy and the Socratic will of self-knowing saved my soul through Jesus Christ.

***

Whoever lives in the lie is the slave of the lie.

***

All the religions of the world have invented prayers to beg mercy from God.

But none, except the Lord's Prayer who was actually given by God, offers to God the forgiveness of those who made mistakes against us,

although Jesus repeated many times that is of the highest importance to forgive and to be merciful in order to receive forgiveness and mercy from God.

***

Do not name unclean what God cleansed with the blood of His Beloved Son, Jesus Christ.

You must clean the feet of your brothers of the dirt of this world if you want God to cleanse you.

Remember what Jesus said: „It is sufficient if the disciple is like his Teacher".

If He cleaned our feet, we must also clean one another's feet.

***

In our prayers, we do not need to remember God to be good and merciful.

In our prayers, we must remember ourselves to be good and merciful and all-forgiving, and to God, we need only to give what is justly His, THE RESPECT.

***

118

You complain that you are poor, but you despise the infinite riches of God, which are in the Spirit of Jesus Christ.

***

We become perfect by admitting our imperfections.

***

The voice of the mad collective consciousness that always doubts God, and doesn't want to see its own mistakes, it is the nature of darkness.

It is true that I make mistakes, and it is also true that the men are not God or good. Only God is good.

***

The light shines into the darkness, and the darkness never put it out.

When you speak the Name of God the Holy Spirit will come.

Be not, against the Holy Spirit of God, be not against the Truth.

***

To love God means to receive His love.

God loves you, be not an adulterous soul!

***

Even if you are an ordinary person, to sin against God it is not ordinary in this universe, only on this prison planet. God's Advocate spoke in defense of the honor of God.

Against an abominable ordinary apparently "innocent " sin, the distrust in the Love of God.

***

The Love of the Creator is our judge and savior at the same time.

God is the same yesterday, today and forever.

***

To call the evil good, and the good evil, it is a sin against the Holy Spirit, and it is an unforgivable sin.
**

The blood of God cleanses me and protects me from the flies. Because the flies are attracted by dirt.
***

I love you all with the holy love of Christ.
***

GOD IS MY POWER,
and the true face of God is Jesus Christ.
***

What is your reason?
Or your reason is the lack of reason?
***

Whoever hates the Father, hates the Son also.
Whoever hates The Son hates The Father also.
***

Jesus Christ is the real face of God.
***

Holy Father,
I ask you in the Mighty Name of Jesus Christ, to make me as I was at The Beginning of Creation.
Your will be done. My will is Yours.
***

Heisenberg's uncertainty principle,
postulates that: we cannot know the position and speed of a subatomic particle at the same time. The Heisenberg uncertainty principle does not demonstrate the liberty but the chaos. If a system is unpredictable it means that is chaotic or self-determined. And the Human Species is self-determined. Only God could imagine and determine the self-determination,

He is self-determined, He is the effect without a cause, and we have His Divine Nature, we can also create effects without cause, and this is what unites us, the possibility of creation, of choice.

Freedom is the Profound Nature of God.

We are not biological, biochemical robots. Our consciousness is not an epiphenomenon of our biochemical machine that we call body, our consciousness it is not just a spectator of the movement of our biological machine, that we call the body.

Our Consciousness is Interconnected with the freedom, and they are both Divine in Nature.

***

I know God,

And His True Image is Jesus Christ. Who respects not Jesus, Respects not God.

***

Jesus, I Trust in You.

Jesus represents the morality of the Absolute.

O Blood and Water, that came out from the Heart of Jesus Christ as a fount of Mercy for us, I trust in You!

***

"Remember My Passion, and if you do not believe My words, at least believe My wounds. „Jesus Christ, Saint Faustina Journal

***

Is your name in the book of acts?

***

The Blood and the Word of God cleanse me and protect me from the flies.

Because the flies are attracted by dirt.

***

A truth spoken can be crucified by the ones who do not like the truth.

When the truth is too holy to be said, you just let the reality to judge the liars.

Jesus Christ is the Word that came out of God, and the Word of God is the Truth.

***

THIS IS THE CONDEMNATION THAT THE LIGHT HAS COME
INTO THE WORLD BUT THE PEOPLE LOVED DARKNESS
RATHER THAN THE LIGHT, BECAUSE THEIR DEEDS WERE
EVIL.

***

Name not unclean what God made clean.

If you do so, you sin against the Holy Spirit, and this is an unforgivable sin.

***

Only a perverted soul fears the Holy Spirit.

***

We must be like the victims from the beginning, that were defended by God.

We must forgive, and we must let God defend us.

We must not let ourselves provoked into making evil.

God is just, and His justice is perfect.

We must let God, make a perfect justice, in this way we shall be perfect, like the victims from The Beginning, of a divine nobility.

***

If you consume dark art that means you're a "goth ", a troubled teenager.

If you create events, if you search for people that produce psychic pain, it is the same thing, the same mental mechanism.

It is because "this world likes darkness rather than the light "like Jesus said to Nicodimus.

The death and sex sell the best.

What tells that about us?

That Jesus was right, who comes not to Him it is that he or she prefers darkness rather than the light.

The light is the Truth and this world like the self-deception.

***

We learn from mistakes; we must avoid the deadly mistakes. (see also spiritual death).

***

The tree of life is The Cross and His Fruit is Jesus.

Accept Him, and you will be accepted back into the lost paradise.

***

The judgment will begin at the House of God.

***

The cloak of the angels of light it is the faith, the good deeds, the honest love,

the hope of salvation of this world, the word of God,

the humility in front of God, but not the humility in front of this rebelled world.

I call the Mighty Name of Jesus Christ and the Holy Spirit of God!

***

I love the angels instead because they love me with the love of God.

***

God is every day with us, and we live in Paradise.

But He cannot be crucified and worshiped at the same time.

Jesus, it is the same yesterday, today and forever.

And the human species it the same as 2000 years ago, is crucifying God, and God continues to love us.

He cannot protect us if we are busy putting nails in His hands and feet.

***

"Jesus is the same yesterday, today and forever."
Apostle Paul (Hebrews 13:8)

JESUS NEVER LEFT.

WE LEFT HIM.

And God never left Jesus, not even on the cross, especially God would not leave His beloved son alone on the Cross.

When Jesus said: ELI, ELI, LAMA SABACTANI ?

He actually referred to us!!!

We left God and crucified Him, He never left us, not even when we crucify Him because He loves us. Return to Him, Return to God Return into the light.

Call His Name, and the His Holy Spirit will come, only pay attention not to crucify Him.

Receive His Holy Love that comes with the power of light, the divine protection and divine superintelligence in the Holy Spirit.

***

To speak in the Name of Christ, you must receive His authority first!

***

Purify yourself through repentance, and forgiveness, before asking for His Holy Spirit.

***

God loves the Human Species so much, that He wants to transcend it into a God Species.

If you only knew the love and the nobility of God and His Holy Angels... God bless you all!

***

A single filthy thought can spoil all your mind.

If you want to enter the mind of God, you must think with the thoughts of God, and we know that God's true image is Jesus Christ.

***

Antivenin:

God loves you.

God defended the victims from The Beginnings.

Realize that, and you will enter NOW into paradise.

***

Even bad publicity it is still publicity, every marketing person, knows that.

This is the reason why I say to you: speak not of the evil spirits because you will call them.

***

God loves the Human Species.

Jesus Christ is the evidence.

When God descended on this prison planet, the inmates crucified Him, and He proved the infinite love that He has for this decayed humanity.

***

A house divided cannot stand.

To try to divide the House of God it is an unforgivable sin.

Any punishment it is justified against such sin.

And this book is a weapon against the divider, a sword of light.

The strongest weapon against the divider it is the lack of naivety and the word of God.

***

Trial and error.

We function by the algorithm of Trial an Error, if we do not recognize our errors we become dysfunctional.

***

The nostalgia of sin felt sometimes by the angels and always by the mediocre.

We sin because of our mediocrity in good deeds, the self-deception which follows the sin, builds a pathological arrogance.

***

Who believes not God, makes Him a liar.

In God, we trust.

Only in God.

***

The word of God makes you clean and Free.

***

I have to convince my brothers to Trust in Jesus if they want to get out of hell. To trust the Power of Light.

***

The Holy Spirit will not protect the Perverted Spirit.

***

My Faith saved me.

If I am politically correct, I only have a temporary advantage, if I am divinely correct I will have peace for eternity.

***

I will always respect the morality of Jesus Christ.

***

The nature of darkness is the self-deception.

A dark mind doesn't want the light because doesn't want to see its mistakes.

Here on this prison planet, Earth, there only a few who truly love God because God says always the Truth.

The man created a web of lies, in which everybody loves to believe.

Our favorite self-deception is that we are good. We are not, ONLY GOD IS GOOD. Every prisoner, from Prison Planet Earth, thinks he is not guilty.

The first step to free yourself is admitting the Truth.

The mandatory second step is repentance. Guilt is good. Only the darkness teaches the unrepentance, the rejection of guilt. The psychologists who teach the rejection of guilt are with or without knowing it, tools of the darkness.

The final step to paradise: you must forgive your brothers. And then God will free you through Jesus Christ.

***

To know God, you must first know yourself.

You must have an Absolute sincerity with yourself in order to know the Absolute.

***

In a world of the blind, it can be empirically considered that the light does not exist.

***

"I tell the Truth, that's why you do not believe me "Jesus Christ.

***

And I walked in paradise and I saw a rose surrounded by weed.

The next time I would like to see a field of roses surrounding a weed. Think only with the thoughts of Christ if you want to be really happy, Because the beautiful thoughts give beautiful feelings. I tell you the Truth: The thoughts of Jesus are the thoughts of God. Where is your heart, there is your treasure.

***

The morality of Absolute is the morality of Jesus Christ. The true face of God is Jesus Christ.

***

If God forgave me, I must also forgive my brothers.
***

The thoughts I tell you are priceless because they give Life in The Holy Spirit, there are thoughts for that I have fought greatly against the darkness.

My 24 karat DYMOND is this thought: GOD PROTECTED THE VICTIMS FROM THE BEGINNING.

And after I had this thought, God descended into my house and loved me with an infinite holy love, and

I have said to Him, that I do not DESERVE all this love, And He told me -telepathically –

I LOVE YOU BECAUSE YOU WERE BORN.

God loves you also because you were born,

and this book's purpose it is to teach how to open your mind and heart to receive the Holy Spirit.
***

God loves you, but you are unfaithful.

Jesus loves you, but you are an adulterous soul.

The Holy Spirit Loves you, be not a spirit of deceit!

The ultimate form of deceit it is the self-deceit.

And the preferred illusion of the Humankind it is that it is good.

John said very well:

whoever believes has no sin deceives himself and makes God a liar. That's why I said also that the greatest sin it is to say you have no sin.
***

The ones who are the protectors of the Truth will be in truth protected.

The ones who deceive themselves and others will be deceived. And the light shines in the darkness and the darkness has never put it out.

And God separated from the beginning the light from the darkness.

***

And Jesus was crucified in a place called Golgotha (the place of the Head).

We crucify God daily in our minds, by our misjudgment and He continues to love us with a slight smile on His Holy Face. I know that by revelation.

***

God never left us, we left Him.

For what?

For the illusion of being morally superior to God and His angels. This is a profound truth, and this is the origin of all the evil in the world.

***

The morality of Christ is the morality of God.

Who despises the morality of Christ, believes that he is morally superior to God, which is an unpardonable sin, a sin against the Spirit of the Truth.

Who tries to divide the House of God will never be forgiven.

***

God loves you.

God defended the victims from the beginnings.

***

-What is The Beginning?

-The Beginning is the first civilization.

-Who are the victims?

 -The angels

-Who are us?

-The aggressors from the beginning.

129

We were the aggressors.

The true victims were defended by GOD.

-What happened with the remains the first civilization?

- They remained in the light.

-Have they also a material world? their own planet, where everybody has a perfect morality, where all love each other with a sincerely holy love, and they love God with all their minds, hearts, soul and power?

This planet is of hate and lie, and of the lying love.

***

What it is politically correct, can be morally wrong. War is morally wrong but politically correct but that's no excuse in front of GOD.

***

-Can you mathematically demonstrate the Love of God?

-Can you teach the snakes to love?

In the same way, a snake misses, a part of the brain to understand emotions (it is called a reptilian brain in biology).

In the same way, some of us cannot understand the love of God. Emotions are processed by the neocortex which is more complex in nature.

***

Respect God with all your mind, and you will enter in paradise.

If you do Not respect God, you will Not enter in Paradise, and to respect God means also to do His Good Will, and the revealed Will of God is Jesus Christ.

***

God Never left Jesus,

We are the ones who left Jesus and God.

***

The love of God,

The majority cannot feel it because they are just flowers who are too young and they didn't yet open up their hearts, or they are too old...already dead spiritually.
***

We love God when we accept and recognize His Holy Love.
***

There isn't a stone that God cannot break, there isn't a heart that cannot be humbled.
***

Don't curse the darkness, just turn on the light of prayer and fasting, and of the Holy Word of God.
***

The love of God is the power of God.
***

The Holy Love can carry any cross.
"Eli, Eli lama sabactani?
My God, why did you left me?" (Mat. 27: 46)
God never left Jesus,
Actually, Jesus spoke to us, to mankind.
Jesus answered them: Is it not written in your Law, 'I have said you are gods'?
(John 10:34)
We left Him and crucified Him. Return to your first love, Return to God.
Return to the light!
We are gods also, Atman equals Brahman, we are God's children, conscious, self- determined and immortal.
We are pieces of God, light from the light of the Father of lights.
We exist because the Holy Love of God sustains us into existence.
***

Any soul that despises the Intelligence of The Creator of the Infinite Universe no longer belongs for this mad arrogance to the Human Species.

***

"Now this is eternal life: that they know you, the only true God, and Jesus Christ, whom you have sent." John 17:3.

***

The truth will make you clean. The truth is the word of God.

***

God cannot protect you if you are busy crucifying Him in a place called Golgotha. (in your mind).

***

"They have no excuse for their sin "John 15:22

***

"The deeds that I make with the authority of my Father, Speak about me "Jesus

***

"Believe in the light to be children of the light" John 12:36.

***

"The Glory of The Father it is shown up through the Son."

***

"The Father will give you anything you will ask in my Name." Jesus Christ

***

I am with the feet on the ground, but with my heart in the sky.

***

"Unfaithful souls, you do not know the Holy Spirit wants you with jealousy for Himself ?"

Jesus loves you but you are an adulterous soul.

***

Return to your first love: the Holy Spirit.
***

The antivenin is the word of God.
***

God knows us better than we know ourselves.

The humankind doesn't want to know God, because the humankind doesn't want to know itself, and what has become by leaving the Holy Spirit.
***

God loves you but you are an adulterous soul, that despises His Love, His Morality, His Holy Spirit, even His Forgiveness.

The spirit of men it is pathologically petrified in arrogance.

The victims from today are yesterday's aggressors, and victims from the beginning were defended by God.
***

The banality of blasphemy, the banality of evil.
***

Any retarded soldier after he killed women and children a few miles from home, when he returns believes he is a saint.
***

"The wisdom is proved just by all her children." Luke 7:35.
***

How morally superior mankind believes is to God... shame on this post-human species.

It is always a revelation to make God's will...
***

You were made clean by the thoughts of God, and by His blood.
***

Whoever denies the existence of light is a volunteer blind.

***

"When the Son makes you free, then you are really free." John 8:36.

***

"Or do you despise the riches of his goodness, forbearance, and patience, not knowing that the goodness of God leads you to repentance? "Romans 2:4

***

To enter Paradise, you must first repent and forgive.

***

Not every criminal who knows he is evil will be freed.

Not every murderer and a liar who knows he is a hater and a liar will be forgiven and liberated.

Not every prisoner who knows he made wrong will be freed. Only the prisoners who are really sorry and who forgive what the other prisoners have done to them.

And God loves with the same Infinite Holy Love all the prisoners of His Justice.

***

Jesus loves you but you are an adulterous soul.

***

A blind man can deny the existence of the sun, but the blind man exists because of the sun.

***

If you trust the anesthetist you will have no fear of anesthesia.

If you TRUST GOD, you will have never fear.

And the trust is the measure of respect.

***

"There is no fear in love, but the perfect love casts out fear. " 1 John 4:18

***

The beginning of wisdom is the fear of God, the completeness of wisdom is the Love of God. There is no fear in love and no darkness in light.

And the perfect love cast out fear and the light shines into the darkness and the darkness never put it out.

And God is light and there is no darkness in Him.

Be love and light to stay in God, because God is light and love, and He separated the darkness from the light from the beginning.

***

Thinking is not only allowed, but mandatory to stay in the light.

Love God with all your mind.

***

Jesus said: „Love one another as I loved you." John 15:12

I love you all, with the love of Jesus, because the love of God, who is in Jesus, is our Judge and Savior at the same time, it depends on our character.

Our character finally judges or saves us through the perfect love of God.

***

Only small people cannot forgive small mistakes, And the noble people can forgive big mistakes.

But the sin against the Holy Spirit shall not be forgiven, that means that the sin against the Spirit of the Truth (the spirit of Science) it is abominable.

A House Divided cannot stand.

Sin not against The Holy Spirit of God, sin not against the Truth!

***

Jesus said to them, "A prophet is not without honor except in his own town, among his relatives and in his own home." Mark 6:4

***

God's Advocate, means to be ready to offend people in order to defend God because I know people love to offend God. And this is the perversity of the Spirit of Deceit, of the Perverted Spirit, the enemy of God.

***

-What is The Beginning?

-The Beginning is the first civilization.

-Who are the victims?

 Who are us?

-We were the aggressors.

The true victims were defended by GOD.

-What happened with the rest of the first civilization?

-They remained in the light.

-Have they also a material world? their own planet, where everybody has a perfect morality, where all love each other with a sincerely holy love, and they love God with all their minds; hearts, soul, and power?

-This planet, Earth, is a prison planet, of hate and lie, and of the lying, perverted love.

***

What it is politically correct, can be morally wrong.

War is morally wrong, but politically correct, but that's no excuse in front of GOD.

***

THE TRUE IMAGE OF GOD IS JESUS CHRIST.

***

The love of God, judge us, and He loves us all with the same love.

***

I made a sacrifice to come to the Light of Jesus Christ: I sacrificed myself. Because what it is the use to conquer the world but to lose yourself?

***

To have the eternal life you must know all the time that only God is Good.

***

Only small people cannot forgive small mistakes
And with small people, you must be careful not to crush them in your feet.

***

You shall not name unclean, what God made clean, with the blood of His Holy Son.

***

I am protected by the blood of God.

***

The evil lie is a sin against the Holy Spirit. The lie of the heart is the perverted spirit, the enemy of the Spirit of Truth.

***

Most men consider themselves "just".
They reflect the behavior of the others.
If you are aggressive, they will become aggressive.
If you smile they will smile,
If you are good to them, they will be good for you.
It is a reactive behavior, mirroring.
If you are full of fear they will be full of fear also. If you love them they will love.
You must see yourself as you really are. Full of fear, love or hate.

***

Your will be done, My God.
I prefer the criticized by God, rather than to be praised by man.

***

We learn by trial and error, if we do not recognize our errors we will never succeed to return to the Light.
***

"And forgive us our trespasses, as we forgive those who trespass against us."
GOD SAID WE MUST FORGIVE TO BE FORGIVEN WE MUST
BE MERCIFUL TO RECEIVE MERCY, THE MAJORITY IGNORE THIS TRUTH.
***

I oppose deception, I am the advocate of God.
***

Jesus had the courage to say the truth.
***

You should ask your subconscious what he believes about God.
***

The antivenin:
God loves the Human Species,
But the Human Species is unfaithful to the Spirit of the Truth and cheats Him with the spirit of illusion.
***

EXO DEUS (lat.)
We came out of God.
We are free and immortal consciousness, we are souls from the Soul of God.
***

With the feet on the ground and the soul in the sky, this is the way of invincibility on Earth.
***

Above the clouds, the sky is always blue.
Name not unclean what God made clean, with His Blood.

***

With this book, I will seduce you back into the light.
***

It has no importance what you believe about me, but it is of the highest importance what we believe about God.
This opinion is our judgment.
***

Whoever doubts God's morality, proves that has no respect for Him, and surely where is no respect cannot be love.
***

I love you with the holy love of Jesus.
I bless you in the Name of the Father, the Son, and the Holy Spirit.
***

Show me please, my Lord, my God, my Creator, where I make mistakes, to correct myself.
We function by the algorithm of Trial and error.
***

An A.I., independent and adaptable at new situations can only function by the algorithm of trial and error.
The majority that sees their errors will correct themselves.
The Human Species is a Natural Intelligence, that sometimes is too arrogant to see its errors, that's why it persists in them with catastrophic effects for this planet.
***

But this is to fulfill what is written in their Law: "They hated Me [like animals] without reason". When the Advocate comes, whom I will send you from the Father —the Spirit of Truth who goes out from the Father—He will testify about Me... John 15:25
***

I will teach you a parable:

Let's assume that you are a billionaire, a CEO of a multinational corporation, and you have some employees that broke the law.

-Are you guilty for their crimes?

-No, obviously.

***

The Infinite Holy Love of God, is our Judge and Savior, at the same time. Be Holy!

To God you do not need to beg, to God you need to thank. When you suffer the most, you must say:

THANK YOU, GOD, FOR THE RAYS OF LIGHT OF THIS DAY.

When you think, you have and are nothing, if you only knew to be grateful to God, you will realize that you have and are everything. If you will thank God sincerely, you will realize what I have realized, that we are living in Paradise, but the ungratefulness and arrogance create the inferno in our minds.

A madman who looks at the sun through stained glass can believe the rays of the sun are dirty.

I tell you the truth: our thoughts are dirty, that's why we cannot see the real beauty of this world.

The concept of praying should be replaced with the concept of thanking. And the habitude of begging for mercy should be replaced with being merciful.

And the dogmatic attitude to demand God's forgiveness should be replaced by sincerely forgiving.

God is Absolute in Goodness but we have forgotten to sincerely thank Him. God being Absolute in Goodness, the Mercy already exists.

We must really thank Him, be merciful and sincerely forgive.

***

If you believe that God suffered like a man on the cross, I have a question for you: how much darkness do you believe is necessary to defeat the light?

The light will always overcome the darkness.

And Jesus suffered like God because He is God.

And God is the light which is unapproachable by any dark soul. The love of God is the supreme analgesic.

And he who cannot understand the love of God proves that he never truly loved.

To understand the love of God you need only to really love anybody at least one time with sincere, holy love.

This is all that God demands.

And the justice and the love of God do not contradict themselves.

To understand and receive the Holy love of God it is mandatory to have loved once anybody with holy love.

And, the mercy, forgiveness and the justice of God do not contradict themselves, Because Jesus said:" Happy the merciful because they will receive mercy ,,and " forgive us as we forgive ".

We all need to remember this idea in our prayers, God wants real worship in spirit and in truth, and I know that we all agree that the hypocrisy of the clerics destroyed the western Church in the same way the Pharisees, intellectuals and soldiers crucified the Body of Christ.

***

I searched a man with a candle during the day, like Diogenes, and I found Him in Heaven, his Name is Jesus Christ.

Ecce Homo (lat.) Behold the Man: the real face of God and His angels of pure light: Jesus Christ, the one who loves me simply because I was born, and He loves you all with the same love.

Receive it! Be not cynics, like the old Diogenes!

Despise not my discovery because you offend God more than you offend me.

***

God loves the Human Species but the Human Species is to Him unfaithful.

God loves you but you are to Him unfaithful, like an adulterous woman to her husband.

Jesus loves you but you are an adulterous soul.

***

"But like a woman unfaithful to her husband, so you, Israel, have been unfaithful to me," declares the LORD.

Jeremiah 3:20

***

My work is to make you believe that God really loves you. When you will realize that God is not only Just but He is also an infinite ocean of pure Holy Love, you will enter by the gates in paradise.

This is my work, this is the work of God's Advocate.

I will cure this sick collective consciousness that distrusts the love of God.

I will cure you and we shall all meet again, my old friends and brothers from The Beginning, in Paradise, in the Light of our Divine Father.

I am confident because I am not alone in this, but God is with me, and there is nothing that can fool me to be against Him.

God is with me, and I will be for Him for eternity.

God and Jesus Christ, are the Highest Power, and they mean everything to me, and I was made one with them through the Holy Spirit.

GOD IS MY POWER.

Glory be to God in the Highest!
God defended the victims from The Beginning.
God loves the human species.
God loves you because you were born.
***

The banality of evil is more dangerous than the obvious evil because we think is innocent.

We are all fallen from God's grace.

Nobody is good, there are no innocents on this Prison Planet. Only when you see and condemn the darkness in you and in others can you see and glorify the goodness of God.

The problem with this species is that it considers itself good.

We are not, only God is.
***

Meditate on this verse:" forgive our trespasses as we forgive those who trespassed against us "(Lord's Prayer).

The best defense is not the offense, but the forgiveness.

If we forgive all, we will be forgiven for all our mistakes, and we will be protected like the angels, like the victims from The Beginning.

The greatest sin is to say you have no sin.

Trust in the love of God, in His Mercy, and in His justice.

It is only just to forgive before we are forgiven.

Jesus said: „But if you do not forgive, neither will your Father who is in heaven forgive your transgressions" Mark 11:26

All the dogmatic forget that, in their prayers.

They only try to force God to forgive their unforgiving souls...

Sorry, think better my friends...

Thinking is not only allowed but mandatory to enter and to remain in Heaven, and all that despise the morality of forgiveness they will be saturated by the justice.

***

The victims from today are yesterday's aggressors,

And the victims from the beginning were defended by God. We can free ourselves from the prison of sin If we repent and forgive...all.

Without repentance and forgiveness, from our part, will be no salvation.

God protects His children from the unrepeated sinners (haters, liars, conspirators, the creators of the web of lies, etc.).

Would you receive an unrepentant criminal in your House, near your children?

But I know you think yourself clean...so you think you do not need a bath.

God is so good that he actually receives killers near His children, in His House, but the killers must first repent and forgive all their transgressors ...

And the good news is that: God cannot be lied to.

***

The truth the delight of angels and the pain of men.

A true angel is holy, a lying angel is perverse.

There will never be peace, between the holy, sincere love of the Holy Spirit and the lying, perverse love of the perverted spirits, that lie even with their hearts.

God separated from the beginning the light from the darkness.

There will never be peace between the Spiritus Sanctus (the Holy Spirit, The Spirit of the Truth, Parakletus, God's Advocate, the Protector of all that live in the light

144

of God) and the Spiritus Perversus (lat. The Perverted Spirit, the Deceiver).

The love of God, because it is Holy, it is the delight of angels and the judgment of the perverted spirits, that deceive even themselves.

***

My purpose is not necessarily to convert the persons of other religions, but to convert Christians to Christianity, and only that it would be sufficient to save the whole world.

***

To call the darkness light, it is an unforgivable sin, it is a sin against the Holy Spirit.

Jesus Christ, the Man who forgave his murderers, said that the sin against the Holy Spirit it is without forgiveness, it is a sin greater than murder, and to call evil good, it is such a sin.

The ones who are blind to the darkness from others are the ones who deny the darkness from themselves, and they will become victims of their own self-deceit.

To say that abortions are good, just because they are an exercise of freedom, it is to call evil good, and the darkness light, a sin that The One who forgave and loved His murderers, said it is until the End of Eternity, without forgiveness.

***

The best defense is not the offense but the forgiveness, because if you sincerely forgive all you will be forgiven for all, and you will be protected by GOD, like the true victims from The Beginnings.

So, the most intelligent thing that you can do in life is to sincerely forgive.

You must intelligently understand that you are not without sin, as you like to believe, and you must understand also God is invincible.

145

***

To make the great deeds of GOD, the miracles, the healings, to walk on water, and to stop the storms, you must make the little deeds first, the little GOOD DEEDS of the ordinary day.

***

"Do not despise the small beginnings, for the Lord rejoices to see the work begin." Zechariah 4:10

***

If a friend comes to you in the night to ask for bread, you will surely give him the bread, as Jesus taught us in the parable.

So, any prayer that you ascend to God will be accomplished,

but you must come to God as His friend, NOT HIS enemy.

***

May the Power of Love of Jesus Christ, give you happiness and light.

May the Power of Light of Jesus Christ, give you wisdom and love.

PRAYERS

Calling the Light

And the Holy Spirit and I, say: come here Lord Jesus,
come here.

Come here and heal the sick and the blind.

Clean us with your Holy Blood and The Holy Water,

Which came out of your pierced Heart in the Day Of
Your
Crucifixion,

by the ones who you love so much.

Every day is a day, in which we crucify God,
by our mistakes and by our misjudgment,
in our minds and hearts.

And He continues to love us,

He always loved us,

He always loves us

And He will always love us.

Return to Him,

He will not punish you,

if you come with a humble heart and you forgive your brothers.

He will teach how to really love one another.

Lord's Prayer

Our Father, who is in heaven,
SANCTIFIED be Your Name,
May Your Kingdom be fulfilled
May Your will be done,
On earth as it is in Heaven.
Our BREAD / FRUIT /
THOUGHTS TOWARDS LIFE.**
Give us day by day.
And forgive us our sins,
Just as we should forgive our debtors.
And do not bring us to ***JUSTICE.**
Rather deliver us from evil.
AMEN

***According to the original Aramaic version.
L'nisayuna = trial/ JUSTICE**
** BREAD=THE LOGOS=JESUS=THE TREE OF LIFE=THE WORD OF GOD

Abbun d'bishmayya / Our Father' (Lord's Prayer) in Jewish Aramaic

Abbun d'bishmayya,
yitqadesh sh'makh!
titey malkhutakh;
tihey re`utakh –
heykhma d'bishmayya,
keyn af be'ar`a. lachman d'me'ar`a,
hab lan yoma deyn umachra.
ushbaq lan chobayn,
heykma d'af sh'baqnan l'chayyabayn.
ve'al ta`eylan l'nisayuna,
ela atseylan min bisha

Our Father, Who is in Heaven,
Sanctified be Your Name;
May Your Kingdom be **fulfilled**;
May Your will be released –
Just as it is in heaven,
So also upon the earth.
Our bread, which is from the earth, Give us day by day.
And forgive us our sins,
Just as we should forgive our debtors.
And do not bring us to trial/**JUSTICE**,
Rather **deliver us** from evil.
AMEN

PRAYER

I begin by thanking you Holy God for the rays of light
of this day.
Thank you that you created me and brought me into
existence.
I came out of you, from The Father of Lights and Holy
Love, and I exist because you support me into existence.
Glory be to God in the Highest!
Today I want to forgive every person that sinned
against me with the thought, with the word or with the
deed.
And I repent for the day's mistakes.
Thank you, Lord.
I know that the blood of your beloved Son will cleanse
me if I cleanse also my brothers because all the souls
came out of You, Holy Spirit of God.
God loves us because we were born, and we all were
born of God.
God defended the victims from the beginning.
In the Name of the Father and the Son
and of the Holy Spirit.
Amen.

PRAYER

Lord my God,
I thank you for the rays of light of this day

I repent for my mistakes,
and I forgive All who trespassed against me, and I have
mercy of all.

I know that I do not have to beg your mercy and
forgiveness if I give also mercy and forgiveness.
I know that you only are Good and all the world is
wrong.
I know that I do not have to remember you to be good
and merciful, but we must remember ourselves to be
good and merciful,
only in this way, we will receive your mercy.
Glory to God in the highest.
Amen.

PRAYER

Our Father from Heaven,
Respected be your Holy Name,
And Respected be the Name of your Holy Son, Jesus
Christ,
As it is in the Highest, so here on this prison planet,
Our everyday thoughts, give them to us,
And forgive us in the same way we forgive.
And protect us from evil.
AMEN.

PRAYER

I must stay above the clouds,
in the highest, where the sky is always blue,
and where all they say is true.
Glory be to God in the Highest!
In this way, I will be above the clouds, in the perfect
blue sky.
With the feet on the ground and the spirit in the sky.

The Chaplet of Divine Mercy reviewed by non-dogmatic logic.

Make the Sign of the Cross
In the Name of the Father, and of the Son, and of the
Holy Spirit.
Amen.
God's words:
"Repent the Kingdom of Heaven is near!
Blessed are the merciful for they will receive mercy.
If you do not forgive neither your Father who is in
Heaven will forgive your mistakes."
God is crucified for our every mistake.
The imitation of Christ is the imitation of God.
We are the ones who left Jesus, God never left Jesus,
God was with Jesus on the cross through the Holy
Spirit.
Lord Jesus Christ, you were crucified but the Source of
Life came out for souls and the Ocean of Mercy opened
up for the whole world. O Fount of Life, unfathomable
Divine Mercy, I know that you envelop the whole world
and us.
O Blood and Water,
that came out from the Heart of God, Jesus Christ, and
The Holy Spirit.
as a fount of mercy for us,
I trust in You.
The blood and water, that came out from the Heart of
God, defeat the deception.

Our Father, who art in Heaven, hallowed be thy name.
Thy kingdom comes, thy will be done, on earth as it is in
Heaven. Give us this day our daily bread.
And forgive us our trespasses,
as we forgive those who trespass against us. And lead
us not into JUDGEMENT, but deliver us from evil.
Amen.
Apostles Creed:
I believe in God,
the Father almighty, Creator of heaven and earth.
I believe in Jesus Christ, his Holy Son, our Lord,
who was conceived by
the POWER OF THE HOLY SPIRIT
born of the Virgin Mary, suffered under Pontius Pilate,
was crucified, died, and was buried.
He descended to the dead.
On the third day, he rose again.
He ascended into Heaven and is seated at the right hand
of the Father.
He will come again to judge the living and the dead.
I believe in the Holy Spirit,
the holy Christian Church,
the communion of saints,
the forgiveness of sins,
the resurrection of the body,
and the life everlasting.
Amen.
Eternal Father,
I repent for all my mistakes,
I have mercy on my neighbor and on the whole world,
and I forgive all that ever have made mistakes,
make mistakes or will ever make mistakes against me.
Eternal Father,

I offer You:

THANKS for the gift of life.

Repentance for all my mistakes,

The forgiveness of all that made mistakes against me,

The mercy of all my fallen brothers and sisters.

For the sake of Jesus Christ's sorrowful Passion and death on the

Cross,

I repent for all my mistakes,

I have mercy on my neighbor,

and on the whole world,

and I forgive all

that ever have made mistakes,

make mistakes or will ever make mistakes against me.

Amen.

O Blood and Water,

that came out from the Heart of God, Jesus Christ, and The Holy Spirit as a fount of mercy for us,

I trust in You.

The blood and water, that came out from the Heart of God, defeat the deception.

The imitation of Jesus Christ is the imitation of God.

Holy God, Holy Mighty One, Holy Immortal One,

I believe Your words, and I also believe Your wounds.

I trust in your infinite mercy,

that you always have for us and on the whole world.

Eternal God, Your Mercy is endless,

and Your treasury of compassion is inexhaustible,

I know that you always look with kindness upon us,

increase the feeling of Mercy within us,

towards our neighbor and the whole world,

so that, in difficult moments,

we may not despair,

154

nor become despondent,
but may, with great confidence,
submit ourselves to Your Holy Will,
That is Love and Mercy itself.
Make the Sign of the Cross.
In the Name of the Father, and of the Son, and of the
Holy Spirit.
Make the deeds of the Cross also.
Amen.

Made in the USA
Middletown, DE
21 May 2023

31105312R00092